CRITICISM IN THE MAKING

CRITICISM IN THE MAKING

BY

LOUIS CAZAMIAN

PROFESSOR OF ENGLISH LITERATURE AT THE UNIVERSITY OF PARIS

New York
THE MACMILLAN COMPANY
1929

Printed in the United States of America by
J. J. LITTLE AND IVES COMPANY, NEW YORK

FOREWORD

That after so many achievements, and such persuasive explanations of its principles, criticism should still be described as "in the making", not made, may well be set down to sheer perverseness of judgment. The phrase, however, points to an accepted, and indeed a commonplace view. Criticism, like everything else, is in a state of flux; it moves with the times, and borrows some of its hues from the changing world of thought. There does accumulate, none the less, both from argument and from experience, a body of positive results; and the course of critical opinion, with its twists and turns, remains when broadly considered a movement forward.

At few moments perhaps in the past have the prospects of criticism been subject to so much uncertainty as they are now. A sense of readjustment is in the air. New methods are being tried, or, as the case may be, old methods rejuvenated under new names; and more audacious shades are worked into orthodox processes. The stresses that were laid yesterday on some main aspects of research and valuation are obviously shifting; and the issues, which at the beginning of the century might have seemed closed, are decidedly open again.

The "sociological" flood is at the ebb, leaving behind a fertilized soil, a much more definite and a richer notion of the organic relationship between literature and the collective life of groups. The "psycho-analytical" wave has broken, and begins to retire; what will be its legacy to the field of critical doctrine it is yet difficult to say with precision; but that a point of view, a curiosity, a fresh range of problems, and a set of formulæ have been added to the stock in trade of the critic, is at least very probable. Less sudden and less dramatic has been the steady oncoming of the properly "psychological" awareness and spirit; but this has come to stay. The proposition seems established that the problem of interpreting a text is essentially similar to the reading of character; and that in the process the terms into which the unknown quantity has to be translated are and must be borrowed from the personality of the critic. To be psychologically as well as esthetically alive, and to possess all one's own tendencies in a susceptible or actual state, is thus by far the most important requisite of a mind which sets before itself, not only the understanding, but the recreation and the explanation of literary works.

Has impressionism then won its long battle against its several dogmatic opponents? The fight has subsided indeed, and the dust cleared off a little. That in efficient valuation the standards present are not distinguishable from the instinctive preferences of taste, so that nothing is gained by an abstract formulation of qualities which in human experience exist only as concrete, is perhaps a not unfair description of the compromise towards which the current of opinion seems to be setting. Criticism is surely not mere arbitrary self-expression; on the contrary, its subjective approach works out to an objective end. But was ever mere caprice actually the method of an impressionist critic? And was ever a consciousness of standards enough to make a competent judge of books? Standards are nothing in themselves; what matters is the effort that feels after them, and discovers them afresh in each new instance. Now to discover is to recreate them. With all the wide range of individual freaks and fancies, there is a harmony of perception between human minds; and native sense and culture do evolve some relative stability of appreciation. The measure of literary values, in practice, is the rough agreement of trained readers; and the metaphysics of that practical concurrence are foreign to the proper field of criticism.

Meanwhile the philological and the historical—or "scientific"—methods have kept most, if not quite all, of the ground that had been won by their vigorous offensive during the last quarter of the nineteenth century. No one will seriously dispute their claims in their proper spheres; but that they have spheres of their own, and are not the divinely-appointed rulers to the whole empire of criticism, is a view that would have been revolutionary twenty-five years ago; it is on a fair way to becoming quite

orthodox. The correct interpretation of words is
the obvious preliminary to all criticism; and of that
interpretation the science of language holds the main
key. No student of literature is equipped for his
task unless he has learnt to use that key; a more
specialized devotion to philology is not needed of
him. The historical investigation of literary developments did threaten for a time to supersede all other
activities; higher education staked its all on that
austere discipline, and the much wanted reaction is
hardly yet in full swing.. That, none the less, further
progress can still be made and is being made in that
field, is obvious from the brilliant pieces of research
work carried out every year in the spirit of the historical method, and for which new ways often have
to be opened out through fresh tangles of difficulties.
No doubt, the growth of literature in time comes
within the wide domain of the science of the human
past; and a sound knowledge of the facts of development is the foundation for all critical endeavor.
What circumstances, conditions and causes are interwoven with the series of successive literary expressions, and with the substance and the manner
of each of them? This is an ever-present and a vast
subject, well worth the energy and enthusiasm of
historians. But that all students of literature should
be regarded as historians is an exaggerated and a
pernicious assumption. More important still, and
much more fruitful than the problems of origins and
development, are those of content and significance.

What is the human matter, what the artistic value of the work? What individual mind is revealed in it? How can the book be explained by the writer? Those are the main questions at issue; and the help that historical research can bring them, precious and indispensable as it is, is auxiliary, not principal; the just order is reversed if the search for sources, if the preoccupation with literary types or with the genesis of texts through manuscript or book form are given first place. First place they have been given, and still retain it; but their tenure is now disputed, and in jeopardy.

"Comparative" literature, lastly, has come into its own; but its painstaking catalogues of actions and reactions have lost some of the prestige which attached to them a while ago. A weariness has perceptibly crept over the whole matter of "influences". Influences are moral facts, inward changes, and nothing that lives changes but according to the law of its life; a contact that matters is a stimulus given to a budding originality, and what matters then is the originality much more than the contact. Such episodes are expected and inevitable incidents, most often of very little significance, in the story of spontaneous growth and assimilation.—"General" literature, on the contrary, has approved itself better. In an international age, it deals with the problems of more than national scope; whether they concern literary esthetics, or the vast field of distinct and correlated intellectual developments. These it sur-

veys not principally as disturbing and deflecting one
another, but as impulses of roughly similar origin
and direction, harmonized by a growing analogy of
culture, and by the inward ripening of free spiritual
affinities. The notion of rhythms, borrowed from
the physical world, seems not to be out of place as
an index of the recurrent changes through which
collective minds, in their artistic preferences, are
apt to pass.

If the balance of gains and losses were to be
struck, it would be probably found that, in the esti-
mation of an increasing number, the proper values
of literature have long been unduly neglected; that
the study of books for the sake of enjoyment is to
be reinstated in the high place from which it has
been rather ignominiously driven; and that intelligent appreciation, at all degrees, links up with the
deepest and the most truly "scientific" criticism. The
pursuit of the humanities through letters should be
again the staple liberal discipline in universities and
schools alike; and the technique of history may without detriment be reserved for the specialists. The
purely "literary" mode of study is closely connected
with the psychological interpretation of works; and
in the psychology of movements, writers and books
lies the best approach to the greatest problem of all,
the self-determination of group minds in kindred
though original expressions.

Some such reflections and views are embodied in
the following lectures and addresses, the special

themes and occasions of which may not entirely hide their converging lines of thought. To have planned out such a collection, as a dogmatic treatise on the present tendencies of criticism, would have been no doubt an ambitious undertaking. It is perhaps more excusable to take notice of a community of aim and argument which the accidents of lecturing have brought about with no malice aforethought; and to hope that through their related subjects and inspiration, at least, those essays may not be unworthy of publication in book form. The author finds some relief in acknowledging that they raise more questions than they can, within such brief compass, properly discuss, even though his confession should in no wise alleviate his responsibility.

The first six lectures are reprinted from the "Pamphlet" of the Rice Institute, Houston, Texas, where all but one of the six were delivered, the 5th and 6th in May, 1924, and the 1st, 2nd and 3rd in January, 1929. The last three addresses (Parallelism in the Recent Development of English and French Literature) are the William John Alexander lectures, delivered before the University of Toronto on January 28th, 29th and 30th, 1929. The necessary permissions have been kindly granted by Dr. E. O. Lovett, President of the Rice Institute, and Principal M. W. Wallace, of University College, Toronto.

CONTENTS

THE AIMS AND METHOD OF HIGHER LITERARY STUDIES

THE AIMS AND METHOD OF HIGHER LITERARY STUDIES [1]

I

THE LURE OF SOURCES

It is an awe-inspiring thought that the caveman, determined to rear his children according to the light of his mind, made them repeat such magic sounds as tradition had handed down to him—words of witchcraft, tales of war and hunting, or propitiatory homage addressed to the fearful powers of the sky. Those spells had a meaning, more or less clearly caught; they had a virtue beyond the mere value of the terms, in their music and rhythm; the incantation stirred a dim sense of the beautiful, appealed to the imagination, shaped the sensibilities of the young men and women who prepared to take up the duties of life in their turn. Thus began the use of literature as a means of education. The sacred texts would be first learned by heart; then, they would have to be explained, as language had passed on to a new stage, and their form was antiquated; thus the race of grammarians and commentators

---

[1] A series of three lectures delivered at the Rice Institute, Houston, Texas, on January 3, 4, and 5, 1929.

would arise. Next, the full power of the mysterious syllables had to be made accessible to slower or less gifted intelligences, and the critic was born, pointing out beauties and assessing values. Lastly, a more advanced age, feeling itself wonderfully modern, grew curious about those relics of the past for the sake of a bygone time; they were scrutinized for the testimony they bore as to the moods of long dead generations; and the history of literature started on its career. Ever since, the achievements of poets and writers in song and story have held a place of honor in the activities of all schools, colleges, and seminaries of learning. Twenty-five centuries ago, Homer was taught to boys and girls throughout the Greek world; to-day, students over the planet are trained in the scholarly study of texts. Seminars are conducted, theses written, and the number of books about books grows by several thousands every year. So ancient is the habit, so august the whole tradition, that one may well pause in doubt and misgiving at the prospect of looking too closely into the forms which they have assumed of late. However, the step must be taken—not, indeed, with a view to testing the value of literature as an educational instrument: that we are content to accept on trust from the wisdom of all ages—but so as to probe the manner in which literature is taught at present.

Its teaching in universities still somewhat obeys the threefold impulse out of which the crafts of the grammarian, of the critic and of the scholar have grown. It purports to be at once a culture of the mind, meant to quicken the perception of beauty in verbal expression; a formative training of taste, and of the critical faculty; an apprenticeship to research, and to the investigation of the literary past. Such is the order in which those aims have developed; but the modern religion of science has reversed it. History is queen, and the modest nursing of the sensibilities is thrown quite into the shade. Criticism comes in between, bound up with history more or less, and sharing in its dignity. The trend is thus to regard the simple enjoyment of books as only the concern of the secondary school; and we shall but follow the practice of our time, by making the first of those aims the last in our survey.

* * *

In each and every province of our life indeed, the scientific habit of thought has made its influence felt; it has entered into the very temper of our minds. The higher study of literature might have seemed entitled to a position of proud independence; the years are not yet far away, when letters claimed to share with science the privilege of being a value in themselves, and the possession of such virtue as would make them, without any substantial addition or change, an instrument for the shaping of youth. This doctrine is not disowned yet, so far as the lower degrees of teaching are concerned; but in the field of higher education, it has been settled, for half a century or so, that the study of literature was powerless by itself to justify its traditional tenure of a large place in academic exercises. It must needs be enlivened and strengthened with an infusion of a spirit and method entirely alien to its own. To train the esthetic sense, and to deepen that reflection upon life, which an intelligent study of great books can nourish, were not objects of sufficient worth to occupy fruitfully the minds of young men and women who had selected the humanities for their vocation. The necessity to think scientifically was so great and pressing, that to inculcate the habit through other studies would not suffice; it should impregnate all disciplines; and if literature was to survive as a staple subject in higher teaching, it must be brought into line with activities directly controlled by the systematic purpose of organized knowledge.

There was a fair case for the argument; the more so, as science did not pretend to annex the whole extent of the realm it was invading. It only demanded a share; the instrument of letters was to serve its several ends at once; the new use it was put to did not necessarily conflict with the former; on the contrary, a methodical interpretation of books in the same light as other natural facts would broaden the perception of their artistic attributes and human interest. Such was the plea of the many sincere and enthusiastic scholars who were responsible for the refashioning of literary education in its higher spheres. That they made good their promise, on the whole, it would be difficult to deny; and they were themselves signal proof of the value of their faith; erudition and method did not blunt their taste or deaden their sensibilities. But with the passing of time, the revolution effected in scholarship has further developed its consequences; its results are better apparent; the excesses, the seeds of which are contained in each new departure of thought and life, have grown and flourished rankly. It may not be inopportune to point out some of the latter, in the course of a survey too brief not to remain very incomplete.

There are various kinds of scientific knowledge; but some are more typical than the others, as their quality is, so to say, more concentrated and essential. If to know is to organize facts, the organization is the more striking, and seems the more efficient, as it is closer and firmer. The whole history of the moral sciences for a century is that of the attempts which have been repeatedly made, to extend to them the stricter rules and simpler processes that obtained in the world of matter. Again and again, the study of man in his diverse aspects as a moral agent had to free itself from the contagion of practices and methods that clashed with the nature of its object. What is wrong with the higher study of literature, as generally pursued at present, is that it lives upon an antiquated notion of the nature and activity of mind; it keeps repeating, on its own account, errors which have long been exploded in other and more important branches of the moral sciences.

Much is, of course, unexceptionable in the technique which has grown round the editing, deciphering and interpreting of texts. Three generations of scholars have produced a set of recommendations and rules, in the mass certainly not empirical, but which, again, one should not describe as merely deductive. The handbooks that have been written to guide the research worker on his way are most of them admirable; and the doctrine which they teach it not only efficient; it is modest and sane. The genuine student knows that he is not to put his trust entirely in method; a sound notion of the complexity of literary problems, a sense of diffidence as to the results of conjecture, an acceptance of intuition for all that it may be worth, a respect for the spontaneousness of the creative mind, have been instilled into him. But, when all is said, and if the tree is to be judged by its fruit, the technique of literary studies seems in some danger of being hardened and fossilized; it is narrowed, in practice, to a monotonous and somewhat mechanical routine; last, not least, it receives, as a technique, an excessively large amount of attention, and this not in a special department, but through the main body and trunk of higher teaching.

To take up the last point first, it seems obvious that training in that field is of direct utility only to the intended specialist. Let future scholars be taught the lore of research work; they are, after all, but a few. Might it be, then, that the closer exactness which the habit of methodical inquiry can add to literary enjoyment, in itself justifies the time and strength devoted to that apprenticeship by the common run of students? And even if a training in the craft of literary research is of actual use only to the would-be craftsman, might not its universal cultivation be supported on the plea that it possessed intrinsic pedagogic worth?

No doubt, to study a problem for its own sake is a lesson in disinterestedness; to sift truth from error, gauge the value of conjectures, and work out the rights and wrongs of a subject, sharpens the critical faculty, and breeds in the over-hasty temper of the young that prudence, that suspension of judgment, without which there is no sane outlook upon life. And while a methodical habit of mind is not conducive in itself to the greater enjoyment of literature, it induces a mood of modesty and self-diffidence, which should increase the respect with which great books are approached. The research worker feels that he is doing his mite toward the furthering of a large end; should even his own share in the collective task offer him but scant reward, he is cheered—or ought to be cheered—by the ennobling sense of coöperation and self-sacrifice. There resides in the austere activity of the man who acquits himself well of relatively menial duties the spirit of team work, a moral and social influence of no small value.

Thus the orthodox advocate of research. But the flesh of the worker is apt to groan under the ordeal; while his soul, strange to say, shows little sense of the benefit which it receives. What ails him, is the uneasy impression that his most natural appetites are repressed and starved. It might be otherwise; but a training which should offer a wide scope, is too often restricted to one province of its domain. There is breadth, no doubt, in the faith; but it is narrow in its usual application. And just as this fact is of great practical import, going far to sterilize the fecundity of the whole endeavor, it is in itself of very pregnant significance. There, and nowhere else, lies the root of the whole matter.

A connection of some sort will always appear, between the general philosophy of a period, and its characteristic activities in all fields. The higher study of literature was organized during the latter half of the nineteenth century, under the spell of determinist views and an "atomistic" notion of the nature of mind. The main conceptions of psychology have since that time undergone a thorough change; but the influence of the associationist doctrine that prevailed fifty years ago is still strongly stamped upon the craft of the literary student.

At the back of the vast effort which is being heroically pushed forward in thousands of advanced literary courses, there lies an unformulated faith, which might be expressed as follows: all facts have a cause; literary works are products; they are to be accounted for by their antecedents, and can be. Not only are they, in their mass, an aspect of mental and esthetic civilization, to be studied and explained along with other symptoms of intellectual activity; and not only is the history of literature one of the minor moral sciences, entering with other branches into the concrete sociological study of man; but each work individually is to be analyzed into its component parts: it is, when all is said, the result of certain circumstances, which can and should be, as far as possible, investigated and known. The ideal aim of the research student is to gather all the elements that went to the making of a book, just as the chemist analyzes a compound into its constituent principles. When each and every one of those data has been found, the study of literature is on a par with the sciences of the physical world, in the proud feeling of the complete satisfaction which it gives the inquiring mind. It reaches a thorough and final explanation of its object.

Such is the prevailing ideal, under the spell of which literary research seems to have been everywhere organized. Its methods have been consciously worked out, so as to gather all the facts, to establish their connection safely, and to build them up into a system, the inner cogency of which would be identical with the very process which produced the work studied, as the cause produces the effect.

Now the psychology of fifty years ago did encourage and indeed prompted such ambitions and efforts. Most ideas of the mind were then regarded as combinations of simple elements into complex wholes. The law of association was the key to the higher intellectual activities; what more natural, than to take it as the key to artistic and literary creation as well? The view would thus be generally accepted, that a book was the sum of constituent parts—themes, images, notions, suggestions—which the writer had picked up in the course of his experience; life accounted for most of these, and other books did account for the rest. To explain a poem triumphantly was to find out all the influences that had entered into its conception and execution; to know an author was to be acquainted with the origins of all the ideas in his mind; and so literary history was mainly the investigation of sources.

Such an approach to knowledge was beset, no doubt, with difficulties; but it was, after all, under the circumstances, the least arduous to follow; it represented, in fact, the line of least resistance. "Sources" are most often tangible things; it is easier to deal with the obvious elements of a work, than to penetrate into its inner meaning. Thus it is that the higher teaching of literature has been led into the grooves where it is still mainly at present. Two-thirds of its energy are absorbed by the investigation of definite individual origins. To open a learned periodical, or consult a list of theses, is to come across a thick growth of that exuberant weed. A seminar loses half its prestige, unless it is devoted to somebody's influence upon somebody. And the materials with which, apparently, a full explanation of the entire body of literature is at last, some day, to be given, are heaped up with untiring ant-like industry.

But the view of the human mind implied in that position is no longer held, or tenable. The stress has been shifted, from the combination of elementary ideas into complex ones, to the activity of consciousness, the interpenetration of its moments, the originality of qualitative states; and absolute determinism has lost its ascendancy. The spontaneous character of mental life is accepted on all hands. In the light of these new notions, the ceaseless investigation of origins, as it is now conducted, is seen decidedly at a disadvantage.

To ignore that line of inquiry altogether would be of course a grievous excess. In order to comprehend an age of thought or literature, we need to know what broad currents of influence have helped to impregnate the intelligence or the imagination of men with certain themes, conceptions and moods; the interrelation of cultures, groups and periods is an essential chapter in the study of the past. Even with the individual writers and works, the history of their development is part and parcel of that effort to understand, without which there is no knowledge worthy of the name. It may not be immaterial to lay our hands on the sources from which a passage is derived, when the external origin of the ideas or words can throw light on their obscure or ambiguous meaning. There is food for reflection, if not for very varied or enriching thought, in the unexpected places from which the images that throng a poet's work may have gathered; in the strange ways and devious courses of inspiration.

But the value which we should attach to the search for sources is thus seen to be essentially relative, and every case has to prove its claim. It may be, it often is, interesting or useful to know from where the materials of a book were borrowed. The mistaken and exaggerated assumption is that it is always interesting and useful to know it; that we should systematically inquire into the sources of all works ranking as literature; that all such inquiries must smell sweet to the nose of the scholar; that it is possible to bring together all the constituent elements of books in that way; and that there is sanity in the universal effort thus initiated, in the desperate search for the materials which have entered into the whole body of literature, spending on that endless task the best energies of young people with a genuine taste for letters.

In those principles, not often stated fully, but too often acted upon, there hides an erring notion of the aim and method of literary studies. Indeed, one might go so far as to say that the doctrine, in its crudest form, is a soul-killing fetish. It is not possible to gather all the materials out of which a work of literature has grown; and if we could have them all in our hand, they would be only dry bones; the spirit that breathed upon them is everything.

It is not necessarily interesting to know the sources of a book. The inventors of sources usually do not explain much that matters. They do not account for the work of the artist; they do not effectively substitute a mechanical combination of parts for the living act of creation; so far as this act is concerned—and it is the all in all of literature—they do not even, in most cases, throw a revealing or an instructive light upon it. The conclusions of any significance to be drawn from the study of sources are very few. A dozen scrutinies of the kind will establish some elementary facts, all of which we knew before, or which we might have foreseen: the materials of a writer come to him in the most various ways, and those ways may be subconscious as well as conscious; he may take much from sources most alien to his purpose, and most unexpected; there is no limit to the transforming and idealizing power of imagination, working upon the data which memory has gathered; etc. . . Such findings, and the like, are the harvest to be reaped from the investigation of origins; to take stock of them once, and pass on, would be enough. They leave each individual problem very much where it stood; the help which they afford to the study of each is but slight.

It is not conceivable, lastly, that a complete natural history of literature should be put together in that way, with the skeletons of all the works reconstructed bone by bone, all the bones duly labeled and fitted into their places. There will always be lacking, from the sum total of such studies, whatever is energy, vital spark, creative invention; the real substance and manner of growth will not even have been touched upon. There is no accounting from the outside for the genesis of a book worthy of notice; in the process thus sketched out, it is the missing links only that matter. The number of elements that went to the writing of one work is infinite; no reckoning of them will ever be full; those that are most essential are elusive, intangible, cannot be caught and pinned down on the page. A library of research work dealing with sources is an aggregate of inert matter, mostly dead.

Failing the illusory endeavor to "explain" a book by tracing all its materials to some distinct origin, might not the hunt for sources be justified on the plea that the source, when definitely found and compared with the finished work, is a useful index to the author's originality? This is quite another matter, and the problem here assumes a very different aspect. As Professor Manly recently said, "the profit in studying the sources of a great writer is to learn what he has done with his material. Such study of course requires full and accurate texts of the sources."[1] Indeed, to examine the rough sugges-

[1] Preface to the *Canterbury Tales,* edited by Professor Manly, 1928.

tions, whatever they may be, from which the writer started, is part of the artistic study of his work. But what are we to infer from the above guarded statement? That the investigation of sources is profitable only when dealing with great writers, and provided the texts of the sources can be conveniently examined; lastly, that it is useful in so far only as the writer's process of selection and development can be watched at play through that approach to better purpose than through others. If these restrictions are borne in mind, and the study of sources is admitted exclusively on its own merits, it will be found in practice that while the process keeps a place among the normal operations preparatory to criticism, it will have still to be driven from most of the vantage ground which it has so long occupied.

And yet, one can sympathize with the desperate attempt to know how a masterpiece "was made". There is no fault to find, in principle, with the will to take beautiful things to pieces; with the search for the why and the wherefore. The purpose of science is of course sacred. It is the method here that is disappointing, not the quest that is wrong. But if the analysis is to explain its object, the right sort of elements are to be dissociated, and the synthetic force that not only brought them together, but fused them into a whole, is to be recaptured. Now this is no impossible task; and the right sort of criticism— the creative—is able to perform it in such a way as to give us adequate explanations. This will be the subject of the next stage in our inquiry.

Meanwhile, it may be no unfit conclusion to those rather negative remarks, that we should turn in admiration and homage to what appears, at first sight, a signal example of the study of sources at its best. Professor John Livingston Lowes' book, *The Road to Xanadu,* need hardly be introduced to minds in touch with the movement of literature. No methodical investigation could be more thorough; and no reader has dipped into that beautiful work without feeling its fascination. But the lesson of the book is all in favor of our argument. The problem is here definitely carried on to the psychological plane. What the author gives us is a direct view of the transforming power of imagination. We are made a party to the process through which the passive images gathered by experience and reading are infused with an active life, and form into original aggregates. As a strikingly clear survey of the "subconscious alchemy" which lies at the root of invention, no research could be more convincing.

And yet, the book, strong as it is, fails to persuade us entirely. One cannot help thinking that what is amiss with it is just its attempt at the full dissociation of a poem into its constituent elements. In so far as Professor Lowes wants to bring together all the materials of the *Ancient Mariner,* we feel that his net, however masterly the hand that throws it, will not catch the most essential factors of the product. Every single detail may be accounted for; the dovetailing of the themes, images and incidents may be perfect: still, there never was a work of art produced in that way. It is all very well for the critic himself to point out that his analysis is not, cannot be, exhaustive: it is carried away by the enthusiasm of source-finding, and inevitably places the main stress on what remains of secondary importance only. The truly creative principle, when all is said, is the whole personality of Coleridge; that organic, unanalyzable energy did enter into the growth of the poem at every stage; it presided over all the choice of expression. By the side of that deeper activity, the playing and sifting of subconscious images in the recesses of memory must be regarded as more external. And even the other piece subjected to the same test, *Kubla Khan,* did not only sing itself out to a passive spirit; spontaneous and miraculous as this pure gem of fancy may be, it bears the imprint of the mind that made it; really to explain it would be to explain the verbal gifts and the musical instincts of Coleridge's self. Are these in other ways to be explained? Not exactly; but they are to be approached, felt, realized, caught intuitively, we shall see, as far as they can be known at all.

We are not prepared to believe, either, that the study here made of the two poems does reveal to us the precise methods that always govern poetical invention. It sheds a welcome light on the working of an eminent poet's fancy; but hardly any inference can be drawn from it, beyond a few conclusions, of a general nature, which we knew or suspected before. At bottom, the case of every artist, and, indeed, of every poem, is unique; no binding law controls the growth of mental products. Professor Lowes has brilliantly exhausted the possibilities of the search for sources in a privileged instance; his inquiry, bearing on an exceptionally fit subject, most usefully confirms some pre-existing but rather vague ideas as to the psychology of invention. Beyond this, even that most uncannily shrewd discoverer of sources could not go. His book would keep its solid worth, if it did not attempt to say all, where a general lesson is conveyed, rather than particular texts fully accounted for; and the thesis that he does make good, others need not take up after him.

Indeed, the time-honored maxim that the exception is a proof of the rule, might be here aptly recalled. What makes the *Road to Xanadu* one of the outstanding works of criticism in recent years, is the skill, insight and talent of the critic, no less than the glamor that attaches to Coleridgian problems. Whether, after having read that large-sized volume, we are actually possessed of all the ingredients that went to the making of two relatively short poems, is not only uncertain, but most improbable; and to tell the truth, it does not much matter.

From the way along which the organized study of

literature is being pushed further every day, we are thus called back to paths somewhat less ambitious, that do not seem to set out quite so straight toward that goal of scientific knowledge——the discovery of causes. There we may find, however, the living, concrete intelligence of the literary work, the realization of its inner aim; and such a grasp of its development, as will allow us to share in the creative activity of the artist. Could we have that, we need not feel any regret. Not the spectacular dissociation of the work into its elements, not the hunt for its material origins and sources, will give us the illuminating sense of its growth; but an intuitive process, the nature and the conditions of which we must now try to make clear. To understand, on this plane, is primarily the business of the critical faculty. What can the critic do, what should he do, since the search for the historical explanation of works finds its crowning virtue and reality in criticism?

Let us then depart, in respect and awe, from the vast empire of scholarship, whose law it seems to be that the waters of the spirit, there, do not run freely over the earth, refreshing it, but flow underground, so that the devoted band of the source-finders has to dig and burrow for them, with the hope, at best, of a little moisture finally in the desert sand. Before we return, however, to the blessed land of everyman, we may hearken for a while to the pathetic outcry of that anonymous professor, who in the *At-*

lantic Monthly for last September,[1] relieved his overburdened soul. ". . . How heavy has been, and is, the weight of learned volumes, of commentary, exegesis, under which both pedagogue and student must stagger in order to fulfill contemporary academic demands. Month by month and week by week they multiply, tomes, articles, pages upon pages upon the reading of a word or phrase, discussion after discussion upon some minute point of fact, as to the authenticity of a perhaps unimportant fragment or disputed date. . . . If huge tomes, giving an *omnium-gatherum* of all documents, important and unimportant, significant and insignificant, that can in any way be associated with an author, increase and multiply, where will it all stop? . . . Not an assembly of all the phrases he may ever have encountered, paragraphs upon which he may have stumbled through his lifetime, will ever betray his secret. No array of facts, no amount of psychological theory, can interpret that mysterious inner alchemy whereby the stuff of common life is transmuted into gold. . . . How many times, in toiling over note and variant, early reading and later reading, in preparation for the solemn task of teaching poetry to the young, have I felt that way, without confessing it to myself or others! . . ." Alas, what can be done? "Decorum in academic life must be maintained. Yet, for safety, suppressed feelings

[1] "The Pedagogue in Revolt", by a College Professor: *The Atlantic Monthly,* September, 1928.

must come out, in the gospel according to Freud.
. . . Here am I who should at this moment be
getting ready for my seminar, given this year for
the nineteenth time, . . . wantonly wasting precious time. Is it a touch of spring? . . . I am as one
stricken. Should I resign?"

Resign, my sincere and suffering brother? Surely
not; keep on teaching the young, you have the root
of the matter in you. Only be of better cheer; help is
coming. We are many who labor in spirit, they are
few who really prosper and rejoice; let us lift our
voices together, and the walls of Jericho shall fall.

II

THE OBJECT OF CRITICISM

The historians of literature may be the salt of the earth; but by that very token, they are and must remain a small minority. The young men and women who go through the higher courses of literary studies have, most of them, other objects in view. Whatever walks they may intend to follow in after-life, their common desire is simply to be trained in the intelligent enjoyment of books. Whilst only a few among them are budding scholars, all are willing to be given some finer perception of beauty in words. The seminaries of learning are thus faced with a double task: provision is to be made in teaching for the due apprenticeship of the elect, who will carry on the sacred trust and keep adding to knowledge; at the same time, the mental interests of the more numerous flock are not to be forgotten. How can these two aims be pursued together?

It is no exaggeration to say, that they are but ill reconciled at present. The future historian has it all his own way. Courses are conducted, and examinations held, as if all the members of the professional and business classes were to have written, or be able to write, a thesis for the Ph.D. Now this looks very much like a confusion of issues. The historian of letters is a specialist; his training should answer his particular requirements; he must master the technique of his craft, and this is the end to which the discipline of higher studies has been systematically bent. But the common run of students need not acquire that specialized skill. Since what they want is to feel the humanizing influence of great books, the stress laid on technique at the expense of general culture may be, in principle, detrimental to their object; and we know from experience that it is very much so in fact.

The origin of the confusion is not far to seek. It grew naturally out of the search for some common ground, upon which the specialist and the layman could meet. The technical activity of the scholar implies, of course, the normal use of his sensibilities, and his training should make room for their due exercise. On the other hand, it is rightly felt that if the non-professional student of literature is to be capable of an intelligent appreciation, he must go beyond the passive enjoyment of what he reads; he must be instructed, partly at least, in the mysteries of the art, and rub shoulders with the fully initiated. The view is sound; but the arrangement fails entirely, if the cultural virtue of letters is sacrificed to the preoccupation with historical problems, so that the would-be specialist has no chance of keeping his sensibilities fresh and open; and if his own discipline, meanwhile, is inhuman and dry, so that the layman is simply repelled by it.

The common ground on which the scholar and the cultivated man should meet and can meet, is not, as seems to have been taken for granted, literary history; it is the criticism of literature. In the critical functioning of the mind, the technical exertions of the historian find their crowning justification and reality; in it, as well, the unpretending pleasure of the reader of books is refined and deepened. All ranks and varieties of powers, temperaments and tastes are easily brought together in this ample field, where the highest and the lowest are equally at home, because high and low here differ only in degree, not in kind. All sincere reflection upon a text is criticism of a sort; and the best criticism is just that reflection carried as far as it can go.

The critical activity is thus seen to be of the widest and the most varied range. In a manner, it concerns all of us. We shall have occasion to point out that the aim of higher literary studies, as an instrument of education and a formative influence, is to endow every cultivated man or woman with the ability to be, within individual limits, but genuinely, his or her own critic of literature. We cannot, of course, leave it at that. Differences in degree, though not in kind, will at once assert themselves. With some, the function will be exercised to the full; whether or not they make a profession of criticism, their response to the stimulus of a work will be a re-creation of its intent and purpose. With others, the critical act is reduced in scope; these are simply the competent lovers of books. The two species, needless to say, shade off into each other. The distinction is chiefly practical and pedagogical; but under the circumstances, we must make of it the very division of our subject. It is with the former class that the following remarks will deal.

*   *   *

What is meant here by criticism? Not, surely, the magistracy that was once inseparable from the name. To pass judgment in a definite manner, and to assign ranks, is not exactly a superannuated ideal: there will always be a necessity for it; and persons will always be found, who feel equipped for the task, and like to acquit themselves of it. But it would be vain to ignore the fact, that the essential relativity of taste has entered into the very texture of our thought. The values of literature are fixed gradually, by a process of empirical assessment and unceasing correction; each reader, in the democracy of intellectual life, has inherited a share, however unequal, of the privilege which the self-appointed guardians of tradition used to reserve for themselves. There are of course voices of authority, which command attention and respect; in the consensus of opinion that evolves, the sustained power of trained, competent appreciations tells in the long run; the ruin of dogmatic criticism has not spelt complete anarchy. Still, eclecticism has come to stay;

standards have hardly any definite existence outside the reactions of readers, and the belief in a single scale, with unchangeable degrees, has vanished for good. The value of our criticism is measured by the breadth of our sympathies, the acuteness and delicacy of our perceptions; and the hierarchy each of us establishes is valid only for the minds which find their own impressions in ours.

Is the critic thus confined to the passive attitude of impressionism pure and simple; and are the students to be directed toward the cheap and easy ideal of self-sufficient, arbitrary reactions to texts? If it were to be so, we should revert indeed, for the training of youth, to the historical study of literature, as to a discipline that offered at least a promise of objectivity, an outlet for minds bent upon disinterested effort, determined to transcend, if possible, their narrow limits.

But criticism, while losing much of its judicial assurance, and even if we demur at its scientific pretensions, can regain what it lost, and more, in real objectivity of outlook. Its essence is not merely receptive; it implies more than intelligent contact with the stimulus of a book. It is a rich, positive activity, which through sympathy shares in the creative act of the artist. To criticize a work, in the proper sense of the term, is to understand and interpret as fully as possible the urge of energy that produced it; to live again the stages of its development, and partake of the impulses and intentions with which it is still pregnant. This is, in substance, Croce's view, such as Mr. Spingarn, some eighteen years ago, sponsored in America for the first time, with an enthusiasm which no doubt fastened too exclusively on the central sense of a liberating message, and cut criticism adrift with too rash a hand from all its safe moorings in history. When all is said, still, there is no theory more acceptable.[1]

The critic should do, through other means, and more efficiently, what the orthodox historian was after in his quest for sources. No less than the historian, the critic is keenly desirous of explaining the work in hand; to that explanation, he gives his mind fully; in it, all his faculties have a share. A process is thus started, able, on the one hand, to satisfy the legitimate demands of intelligence, of the power that analyzes, links up and classifies things; in close organic affinity, on the other hand, with the simple humanizing enjoyment of letters.

The process might be figured out somewhat in the following way. History, the erudite knowledge of the conditions, the circumstances, the relations—in a word, the externals—of literature, should have a definite place and function in the full cycle of criticism; again, the impressionism of direct, concrete perceptions should have in it its recognized province. Both are necessary, but neither is supreme; they are

---

[1] The text of Mr. Spingarn's address, and the principal pronouncements of authoritative American critics on the issue thus raised, are given in J. C. Bowman's book, *Contemporary American Criticism*, 1926.

adjuncts, preparatory or instrumental, toward the critical act itself. This is of a different order; it is a synthetic activity, which, bearing on the work studied, welds into a central intuition the subjective data gathered by our immediate reaction to the text, and the objective facts supplied by the available historical research.

The end and aim of that synthetic act is to seize from the inside the creative mood of the writer; the complex of emotions and ideas that lies at the core of the work, and from which it originated. This is not merely to divine a purpose, an artistic intent; it is to possess oneself of the very growth and expansion of the purpose into an accomplished reality. Here we have history indeed, but the inner history of a mind, which has obeyed the prompting of self-expression. Towards that full understanding, so complete that it reproduces, at least to some extent, the actual fashioning and shaping of the product, all auxiliary help is of course welcome; and the biography of the writer, the background of literary development and social conditions, the science of language, analytical æsthetics, are called upon to throw as decisive a light as possible on the psychological heart of the problem. No less indispensable is the fine, accurate perception of those values which are the tangible outcome of the author's endeavor.

Thus it is that the critic worthy of the name is really a creator. Judgment, appreciation, intelli-

re inappropriate terms to denote his activ-
aition, sympathy, would be more fitting
f his effort is vigorous, and guided by a suffi-
dy of knowledge, he will fasten unerringly
genetic idea, the *idée génératrice*[1] of the
aot necessarily an idea, but most often an
a mental experience, and almost always an
a of some kind. This is the genuine explanation of the book; in no other way is a concrete relationship established from the effect to its actual
cause. The scientific sense, the craving for the intelligibility of things, is thus most substantially satisfied; and our intuition, radiating out from its central
focus toward each part and aspect of the work, illu-
minates it to our gaze, making it transparent with
an inner light. Our imaginative perception, following the author's mind all along the series of its instinctive acts of will, shares in the decisions, the
preferences, the choice, which are translated into the
characteristics of the work. The major motives and
themes of a book, its leading purposes, and every detail of its construction, manner and style, thus appear to us in their organic unity. Explanation is here
hardly distinguishable from description; the object
studied is presented from within outward, and its
various aspects follow one another in an order not
exactly logical, but natural; everything seems easy

[1] This theory is worked out in M. Pierre Audiat's interesting
book, *La Biographie de l'Œuvre Littéraire, Esquisse d'une Méthode
Critique,* 1924.

and simple, and is so, analysis being nothing but development.

Sympathy is the first condition and indispensable means of that critical intuition; a sympathy prepared, stimulated, enlightened by knowledge; but of all kinds of knowledge, the most profitable here is that which is not abstract or second-hand, but concrete and direct: the data gathered immediately from the self-revelation of the writer in his book. All thus depends on that crucial contact of the critic with the text; there is no activity comparable in mental life, but the concentration of the inventor on his problem, of the creative artist himself on his work. One might even say that the deciphering of a book, or of a writer's personality, by a critic—two processes closely allied, almost identical, though the emphasis slightly varies from one to the other—was a more intensive act than the very writing of that book; in this respect only, that literary composition is reconcilable with a good deal of momentary passiveness, the subconscious powers taking the lead, and the lucid faculties being in abeyance; whilst the heightening of consciousness which the critic's intuition implies—a heightening of the consciousness of *himself,* as identified with another's mental life—is of necessity more clear and connected, making the organic relationships of the work more definite. Criticism mainly consists in realizing, through the power of attention, a complex of intellectual adaptations and sequences which had remained largely obscure in the mind that had lived them first. Hence that paradoxical, but by no means infrequent occurrence: the critic better aware than the author of the purpose and trend of a book. If intelligence were the measure of art, the critic would be the greater artist. But intelligence is not; and the critic, as artist, ranks not indeed necessarily second to the original writer, but somewhere on the same plane; their value being that of creation with one, of re-creation with the other—two perfectly equivalent processes.

Sympathy is a subjective force; it implies affinities which are variable, and may not exist; it has its deficiencies, it is subject to accidents. There will remain, in all criticism worthy of the name, a margin of uncertainty; its working is never safe, as is that of an impersonal scientific experiment. The great critic is the one whose faculty of sympathizing has been almost indefinitely extended, broadened, made more supple by constant exercise, by wide reading, and repeated experience of the unbounded wealth of art. Indeed, the apprenticeship of the critic lies largely in learning how to actualize his sympathetic power to the utmost, in turning to use each and every one of his instincts as the nucleus of a possible personality, the germ of a virtual growth. The critic should be the myriad-minded man. But literature is much more varied and rich than he can be—how could one artist possess in himself, were it only in an infinitesimal form, the personalities of all artists?— and he must have his limits, whatever he may do.

Erudition and knowledge build the background of criticism, prepare and open the way for it, and last but not least, are a test and a trial of its conclusions; but they play a subordinate part in the critical act itself. The historian and the critic, complementary and indispensable to each other, are rarely united in the same person; their efforts will never be entirely reconciled, because they are not on the same plane. That the joint working of activities so different, so alien in their methods and purposes, should always be smooth, is of course not to be expected. Much can and should be done, though, to harmonize them. The critic, at the present day, has not to make allowance for the historian: the tenure he has of his own domain is so precarious, that he could not think of disputing anybody else's possession of other ground. But the historian has to learn how to tolerate and respect the critic.

Such, then, is the process which the great interpreters of literature have always followed; which Hazlitt would live through, and which Coleridge more than once described with the clear-sightedness of the philosopher. But those were men of genius, and the critic need not be one; our reasonable expectation of good criticism would be too scanty otherwise. Mere mortals may, within the bounds of modesty, claim to practice the craft with full, efficient success. The only strict condition is that they should have been provided by nature with an average faculty of intuitive literary perception; that is

to say, of literary talent. There is no good judge of
painting, but he who is gifted with the immediate
sense of color, drawing and picturesque expression,
a sense equivalent to some measure of artistic skill,
and in effect very often accompanied by it. There is
no good judge of books, but he who is not blind to
the intellectual glow that has fused together the elements of a work, and still radiates at its core like
its latent life; and of course, to share in that glow
is to recreate it sympathetically, and to recreate it
is to be able in some measure to create it. When the
operation of criticism is stripped to its essential root,
it supposes instinctive activities that cannot directly
be taught, the power to trace back the product under
study to its last accessible cause, a psychological one.
Many men are born with that ability; and we shall
try to show that most men are endowed with at least
the rudiments of it, so that the purpose of literary
education, from its first beginnings, is just to culti-
vate those rudiments.

But even at the higher level of explicit, full-grown
criticism, much can be done to develop and foster
that intuitive skill. Critics, once born, are trained,
by example and by practice. Here it is that the
courses of colleges and universities stand in a vital
connection with the literature of the country: they
provide, or could provide, the best apprenticeship
for the men who are to give it competent appreciation. The taint of academic origin will not disqualify
those men for the function of open-minded contact

with the new literature in the making, if the special training they have received is not different, in some essential respects, from a cultivation of the creative faculties.

Indeed, on this plane of the full critic, as on that of the mere reader of books, the organized study and interpretation of literary works should provide a schooling for the would-be writers themselves. Entering sympathetically into the genetic process which has produced great books, must stimulate all kinds of productive talents, except, perhaps, that of the genius whose personality discovers itself in rebellion, and with whom independence is the breath of life. We shall be prepared to find that in the future, as in the past, the strongest temperaments are hatched outside the atmosphere of literary nurseries, and are best left to themselves, as they manage generally to be. To the others, whether critics or poets, novelists, playwrights, it is a useful discipline that can show how literary qualities are translated into human terms; how an organic connection is established between a character and its expression; and how an individual mind builds itself up in action and reaction with a moral and social environment. Æsthetic acumen, psychological insight, and the sense of historic interdependence, could not be more efficiently encouraged; and training in constructive criticism is thus no bad school for the future student of art, of philosophy, and for all the varieties of the historian. A precise habit of mind, safety in induction, the fine analysis of moral facts, are part and parcel of the critical activity thus understood.

* * *

But even if it is agreed, that history stands here to criticism as a means toward an end, there must be another field where the relation is reversed, and where criticism leads up to history. The growth of literature through the ages has to be studied and organized so as to fit in with the requirements of knowledge. Now it looks as if the critic's endeavor were strictly limited to the solution of individual problems. Each artistic process is unique; to trace books to their formative ideas and emotions is to write mental biographies. How could the method work out to general conclusions, and a satisfactory ordering of facts?

The answer is, that a principle of generalization, no less fruitful than any other, is contained within the critical activity itself, as here defined. It seizes moods, and their genetic relationships with works; psychology is drawn upon in that inference, and it furnishes the guiding light toward the interpretation of literature. Now, psychology, being scientific in character, tends to be general, even if its laws are not binding; our inner states, whilst always individual, are capable of bearing various and strong analogies; they lend themselves to classification under many heads. Thus it is that the critic is able to utilize his disconnected findings as the materials for a constructive order.

There are affinities of temperament; there are families of writers. No method more naturally leads to a mapping-out of the literary kind, with its species and sub-species, and to a discrimination of their varieties, than that which brings all its power to bear on the biography of books, and thus on the moral history of writers. From this point of view, such notions as "classicism" and "romanticism" are made to reveal the æsthetic reality which they enclose; they are brought into a causal relation with the predominance of certain psychological states. In that way the classifications of criticism are grounded upon the more solid basis of the inner nature of man.

Again, there is thus opened the possibility of organizing knowledge in time, by establishing a unity through the records of the past. When once the results of psychological analysis, dealing not indeed with single works, but with groups and whole periods, are made the object of comparison, it becomes clear that literary movements do not succeed one another by mere chance; the passing from a prevalent mood to a different mental tenor obeys a fairly regular alternation, which is composed with all the unique incalculable elements of circumstance into a pattern of relatively simple succession. One can speak of a rhythm in literature, and with the help of its recurrent though ever modified phases, interpret the relation of each phase to its predecessor and successor. Such large generalizations are not to be pushed too far; they do not resemble in the least the "laws" of the physical, or even those of the biological worlds; still, they afford a clue to the maze of artistic development, and make the history of letters, as well as that of thought, amenable to a measure of logical presentment. In so far as all explanation is not out of place in those fields, those schemes can be regarded as acceptable diagrams, offering the mind a sense of unity and order, whilst leaving a full margin for the original characteristics of each new period and of each new writer.

But whether or not those more ambitious attempts are indulged in, literary criticism, such as it is described here, is a rich and varied activity, appealing to all the powers of our intellectual nature; and it does not leave unsatisfied that craving for connection and dependence between facts, without which there can be the knowledge, but not the history of literature.

For the history of literature there must be; and the literary historian will not be contented with peering into books and writers, joining them in groups and periods, or linking up the periods in a progressive chain of moments. He has to study the connection between each period of literature, and the background of social influences; he has to take into account the parallel developments of language on the one hand—the medium of expression, with its own range, possibilities, limits—of thought on the other, with its prevailing attitudes and fashions.

He has to be aware of the material circumstances that told on the art of writing, from the production and the sale of books to the formation of the reading public and the interrelations of the various literatures. But those subjects have received, during the last half century, a very large share of attention; they have been again and again thought out, methodized, written up; it would be more than superfluous to dwell upon them. Since it is our contention that those various tasks, useful, interesting, important as they may be, are neither the central object of criticism, nor the proper means for the training of the critical mind, we shall only mention them, and pass on. They have too often absorbed the best energy of the best minds among the students of letters; let the specialist be familiar with them, and the layman keep with them a bowing acquaintance; they are not, or at least should not be, the substance of criticism itself; and their formative value for the non-specialist is not such, that he should exercise himself in them for their own sake.

The road seems to be clear for the causal interpretation of books through intuition guided by knowledge. But there remains the difficulty of application. It may be objected, that the ideal which has been sketched out is within the reach only of the gifted few; that it cannot, on the other hand, be put to practice with the economy of effort toward which all habitual operations more or less necessarily tend. One must confess that the method thus briefly outlined seems to provide for no control of regularity, and leave everything to the chance of happy hits; that its routine is not easily formulated; and that as a technique of intuition, relying not on quantity but on quality, not on erudition but on skill, it implies at every step the play of original, creative powers. The objection can be faced with equanimity; it does not seem to be destructive; it does not erect a formidable barrier against the inclusion of criticism in the curriculum of colleges, at the very center of higher literary studies. It is the common faith of pedagogues that the jewel of spirituality can be cut out of the sometimes very unpromising rough material with which nature has endowed every mind; it must be the belief of every professor of literature, that living reactions to books are within the reach of all the young men and women who for the benefit of their culture choose to walk the literary paths. There, and nowhere else, is the animating breath to be found; in no other way will the dry bones of dead authors and distant thoughts be vitalized. That the teacher must give constantly of his best, and radiate out a good deal of the necessary energy, goes without saying. But what teacher ever discoursed of his craft in public, who was not inclined to think with optimistic pride of all the members of his profession? One thing is sure: the young mind whose sensibilities have been called to life in that way, never will lose the ability which has once stirred into being. If the masters of to-morrow are to be able to quicken their disciples, they must be themselves quickened as the students of to-day. The faith is its own proof, and the hope of its votaries will be justified, if sound, by the event.

III

Like the psychologist, the pedagogue is very much with us at present. Our restless world is astir with educational hopes. The teaching and modeling of the young mind is itself being remodeled and reshaped at all its stages, and chiefly at the earliest, that of elementary studies. The spirit of the new methods, some of which are no longer experimental, but have proved themselves, is all in favor of cultivating the personality of the child. Its imagination is to be awakened, its attention appealed to, its faculties quickened, along the lines which nature herself has laid down; the response, such as it may be, of each temperament to each stimulus, is the precious germ out of which every mental development must grow. To correct and curb, if need be, those instinctive powers, to supply, as best one can, their deficiencies, is a necessary but a less essential task; the worth and the happiness of the individual, the well-being and the progress of the species, are all contained in the intuitive susceptibilities of the tender life, that spontaneous promise, which no amount of feeding and nursing can replace if withered or destroyed.

We may regret that the contagion of those subtle,

43

yet simple and efficient methods of approach, should not have spread more definitely to the higher levels of education. What is true of the child is true as well of the young man or woman; the reaction of personality to the stimulus of beauty in words is at all ages the genuine productive influence, that from which the enlargement and refining of mind and heart can be expected; and there is no more real profit to be sought in the study of literature than just that enlargement and refining. If the young people are to be trained in the suppression of self, let them learn by handling some impersonal instrument. If they are to assimilate the rigor of a severe method, and the objectivity of the pure search for truth, let the sciences—those of matter preferably, but the various branches of history as well—be used for that purpose. Algebra or physics are the proper means for the apprenticeship to an inquisitive but dispassionate mood, that follows the working out of an equation or of a problem. If the nice weighing of evidence and the sifting of tangled psychological issues are in question, let the story of the human past—of political, social, economic facts—furnish the texts. But let not the soul-expanding creation of an imaginary world, in which the stature of our kind is the same and yet is greater, be divested of its own special virtue, that of being subject to the laws of quality, not quantity. Literature is precisely the expression and reflection of spiritual man; its humanity is its all in all; to use it as a collection of documents like any other is to rob it of its privilege. One sees the loss; what gain is one to set over against it, if the scientific habit of mind can be acquired as well or better from a hundred other disciplines?

The student who does not set out to be a specialist in the history of letters—that is to say, every student but about one per cent—may then well be liberated from the gratuitous duty to annihilate his natural desire for self-expression. Great books will serve their most substantial end, if they are an incentive to the realization of his personality, intellectual, emotional, moral. His own mind will find itself in the hard exciting tussle with a master spirit —a struggle in which he will be conquered, but out of which he will emerge a fuller man. This psychological interpretation is, we have seen, the very method and object of the critic. Every young man and woman who approaches literature is thus placed in the conditions of the critical activity, and the aim of higher literary studies is to make everybody his own critic. It is only a question of degree, between a Hazlitt or a Sainte-Beuve, and the sincere appreciation of a beginner—provided it be sincere; impressions may be raw, short-sighted, untutored; but they are æsthetically and psychologically productive, if only they are the outcome of actual contact.

The prospect of building the higher study of literature on the foundation of ignorant or naïve reactions to texts, will rouse the skeptical wonder of many, the ironic scorn of not a few. But the democracy of the spirit is no less to be desired, and much more certainly to be attained, than that of political rights; it consists, not in the equal possession of a franchise, one and the same for all, but in the participation, to whatever degree, in the life of the imaginative sensibilities. Here the varieties and differences of individual nature remain indeed supreme; no equality can be spoken of; the hope of the democrat, and the foundation of our faith in letters as a formative principle of culture, is that from every mind, however slow, dim, heavy, encumbered by animality or routine, a spark may be struck out. Although the social sphere of the universities is extending more and more, and takes in a very large part of the national body, the normal student comes to college with the benefit of some educational advantages and facilities; he belongs, most often, to circles where literacy is general, and of long standing; he has breathed an air charged with active æsthetic influences; in the majority of cases, he stands above the lower quality of his fellows in his response to literary stimulus. Such is the permeation of all human material by a subtle diffused essence of civilization, at the present day, that the most unsophisticated sons of the people, the least touched by artificial cultivation, are even sometimes the most vigorous and original, as they are the freshest, in their reactions. No more is needed, to put the higher study of literature on its genuine, secure basis: the assumption that the average man and woman will display a fair measure of sympathy with the spiritual meaning of authors and books. What will be erected upon that basis, depends very largely on the teacher.

The teacher, no doubt, will see difficulties and raise objections; the more stubborn, perhaps, as he has more experience. It would be of no use to ignore the fact that a disinclination to rely much on that personal reaction to texts is a feature of the educational system of some countries; and it would be idle to pretend, that at least in the field of higher teaching, the United States did not show that aversion. Certain reasons may account for the circumstance that the method of appeal to the literary sensibilities is very often fought shy of in this country. Too much should not be made of the fact that for a long time the most conscious effort of the American colleges was to train themselves in a severe objectivity, the example of which was given to the world by Germany; other nations were following that lead, or evolving the same discipline, and still left a freer scope to the personal response of the student. The objective ideal was set up in America with such rigor, only because it answered somehow to the intellectual temperament of many students. And here it is that the incredulous teacher may find some support in the view commonly held of the psychology of young Americans. Most of them, he will say, are tongue-tied when they are asked for genuine literary impressions; put to them a question of that sort, and the sheepy eye will appear; they have no facility that way; the gift of easy self-expression has been refused them; they even look upon it, in principle, with distrust: they do not care to show their feelings. If you try to prevail upon them, and to conquer the shame that paralyzes all open confession of their moods, you will drive them for shelter to ready-made formulæ; instead of being themselves, they will under the strain be anybody else, and repeat mere words.

That state of things prevails often enough indeed; but it is very far from being universal. It seems to correspond rather with the idiosyncrasies of the typical young Anglo-Saxon—and especially the English—than with that of that very different person, the young American. One cannot have gathered any experience of university life in this country, without being struck by the genuine interest which the students of both sexes—and perhaps especially the women—feel in literature. The vivacity, the intelligent eagerness, with which they will respond to appeals of that kind, are very obvious; and not only the best, but the majority, show themselves quite capable of sincere and vivid literary discriminations. It looks as if the responsibility for the future, in that matter, rested decidedly with the teachers, not with the taught. Much could be done to spread the responsiveness more evenly, and make the total absence of it an exception. A complex, no doubt, has with many to be solved; a stiffness of feeling or of language has to be loosened; a free passage has to be opened for the current of self-expression. That will be done easily enough, in a surprising number of cases, if the teacher has the gift, the magnetism, the sympathetic touch; if he has life in him, and can communicate life. The best foundation, of course, for that normal activity of the sensibilities on the literary plane, will have been laid in the secondary school.

Again, it might be objected here, that what the secondary school has done, the university need not be doing a second time. Why duplicate effort in that way? And should not higher studies imply a passage to some more impersonal mode of thinking? This, we hope to have shown, is begging the question; impersonality may be the very thing elsewhere, in other departments; except for special objects, to study literature impersonally is a paradox. Moreover, the interpretation of texts need not assume an entirely new character, when we pass on from school to college; it should only be deepened and broadened. Instead of mere repetition or total change, there must be a linking up in method and spirit, from the lower to the higher. Here, of all places, the growth of the inner man should be paralleled by the smooth development of method; continuity is the breath of the humanities.

The problem is thus seen to narrow down to a matter of practical pedagogy. How is the routine of teaching reconcilable with the sincerity, the surprise, the ever fresh spontaneousness, which mental life on the plane of literary impressions demands? It is not of course to be thought of, that a college class should come to resemble a gathering of literati and wits, each airing his or her opinion of the last best seller, and too much preoccupied with the scoring of a hit, to bother much about discipline, coherence, and concerted effort. But although this happy state of freedom may be approximated in narrow circles of the elect, living under grace, not under law—by which is meant, needless to say, a seminar for the profitable enjoyment, not for the dissection of literature—satisfactory means have long been found to regulate and coördinate, whilst stimulating it, the play of what is perhaps most individualistic in life, the artistic susceptibilities of the young.

The study of texts is the broad common ground on which all programmes and all methods meet. The thoughts, emotions and art of a writer, subjected to group interpretation, give the discussion the fixed permanent basis which is indispensable, whilst allowing a certain margin to the personal reaction of each member. The set of difficulties encountered is such, as to call into play the sense of objectivity, at the same time as the subjective element in every response. An author of standing, and especially a classic (in the general acceptation of the term) represents a sum of values, which the thrashing out of time has definitely enough characterized and circumscribed; by the relatively stable test of those values, the perceptions of single students can be tried, as measuring up to a certain normality, a sanity of taste; and on the other hand, a chance is given to the expression of those original shades, which, however slight, are the birthright of every sincere reader of books, and should no more be repressed than they should be artificially forced and consciously sought after. If anything, it is possible to confess that the teaching of literature has in itself the seed of authoritative dogmatism; most writers studied in class are well worn with the attention of ages; the instructor, however liberal, is apt to regard himself as the representative of a tradition, the holder of a sacred trust, the corrector of erratic freaks; the atmosphere of the classroom, as a rule, would be freer and livelier, if a spice more of tolerance could sweeten literary discussion.

At all events, the time-honored study of texts is not to be dispossessed of its privilege, as the typical and most ordinary exercise. On the contrary, fresh luster, and more substantial rights, should be added to its dignity. It is really and in the full sense the living heart of the whole process of literary interpretation. It should thus be attended and ministered to by all the other activities; the work of a class should lead up to it in every way.

Contact is to be established between the minds of the students and that of the writer, as revealed in a book. The printed page will speak for itself;

nothing can replace, as nothing approaches, the significance of those words selected by a mood eager for realization; but to work back from the expression to the feeling, and from the feeling to the personality, is a slow tentative progress, fraught with dangers, until the short swift road of intuition can be followed; and there is no safe intuition without some familiarity and some knowledge. It takes the mellow experience and the solid learning of the teacher to trace outright the whole in every part, the characteristic features of the man and the artist in each passage. The student is to be guided; and the best preliminary help will be to vitalize and make concrete, as a whole, to his mental sight, the figure which he will, sometime, conjure up for himself piecemeal from the documents. We are here on the typical plane of laboratory, not research work; the final result of the series of operations is as it were given in advance; the beginner has to go through the inductive process in those artificial conditions, so as to fit himself for the independent adventure of discovery. At this stage it is that the life of the author, his manner of being, his dealings with the world, the background of circumstances, social and intellectual, upon which his career and his work stand out, can and should be most usefully presented. This part of the task belongs by right to the teacher; but his set lectures can profitably be supplemented by a course of prescribed reading; and even more serviceable as a training are oral reports, in which the students by turns give an account of some definite biographical or historical problem.

Full preparation having been gone through, the critical edition selected, and the various prefaces duly read, the text itself is to be tackled; and here it is that the peculiar skill France may have developed in the art of literary interpretation has evolved a technique which is perhaps an original contribution to pedagogy, if not to scholarship. The method of the *explication de texte* has received in this country, as in several others, a good deal of friendly attention; it has been more than once described by fully competent observers; on some occasions, by teachers who had a personal and long experience of its routine. It has been, to my knowledge, tried in several American colleges, with very encouraging success. Everything points to the conclusion that the exercise partly embodies the proper essence of higher studies in the literary, as distinguished from the philological or the historical fields. Under the circumstances, it may not be superfluous to examine it once more at some length.

The technical aspect of the *explication de texte* is simple enough. It consists in the union of two things: an analysis on the one hand; a critical interpretation on the other. That the two elements belong to different sorts of mental behavior, so to say, the former being essentially objective, the latter largely subjective, is a difficulty more specious than valid; the association after all is natural, and works well in practice. Its principle is concrete, and pedagogic or artistic; the spirit of science has very little to do with it; but this spirit has very little to do with life itself, and education, when all is said, is the apprenticeship of living. As a first stage, then, the student is expected to give a clear and connected survey of the passage in hand, studying its content, bringing out all the author's intentions, and leaving nothing unexplained in the local development or expression of his thought. This elucidation, naturally, requires the use of some plain methodical devices, such as a genuine division of the passage into its several parts, a coherent classification of the themes, and a linking up of the text, in substance, with the work from which it has been extracted. The qualities of mind most necessary here are not only penetration, judgment, a logical habit of thought, a sense of constructive order; for in fact, there is no accurate comprehension of what an author means, without some share of sympathy with his meaning; it is not possible exactly to probe the special intent with which words and phrases have been selected, unless the reader enters intuitively into the inner motives of the choice. Analysis, on this level, is not a purely intellectual act; except when the passage dealt with is merely rational and argumentative, which will hardly happen but with special categories of writers, the content of the piece will be composed of emotions and images as well as ideas. Now emotions and images are only with difficulty considered in themselves, apart from the personality of the writer. The two aspects of the *explication* shade off into each other.

Shall we say that the analysis is to stop at that? And is quality here not amenable by any means to quantity? Emotion, imagery, words, thought patterns, rhythm, tone patterns: could not those elements of the text be subjected to a more searching, a more precise investigation? They are the very chapter-heads in a significant book, that came recently from that great center of English studies, the University of Chicago.[1] The venture, outstanding in its thoroughness, is typical of many other attempts to reintroduce into the process of literary interpretation itself that quantitative spirit, which ruled so long in the external history of letters, and which we tried to exorcise from the genetic explanation of works. As such, and whatever its ability, the purpose of the book seems to us limited in its fulfillment by the invincible resistance which æsthetic and moral values oppose to all mechanical treatment. But that within a moderate scope the method is not fruitful, no one who has given it a fair trial will be tempted to say. Diagrams and arithmetical devices may be applied to the measuring and figuring out of the instinctive subtle preferences of artists and poets. They will not deaden the soul of enjoyment, and may even enliven it. They are an apt index of

[1] *New Methods for the Study of Literature,* by Edith Rickert; Chicago, 1927.

the modicum of mechanism that the life of the human spirit never goes without. Of course, they should not become an obsession, and hide the reality of the artistic impulse behind a stiff symbolization of its working; their artificiality is not to be lost sight of. Least of all should they point the way to literary creation, as they are not compatible with spontaneousness. But advanced students may profitably learn to adapt those rigid patterns on to the ever not quite exact course of inspiration; by so doing, they will not only heighten the sense of their own ingenuity, but also usefully quicken their awareness of the harmonies and correspondences of verbal expression.

To account properly for the substance of a single page, thus demands a sufficient acquaintance with the purport and progress of the book; and this mental realization of interdependence, this sense of organic wholes, is the main requisite of the second stage, to which we come now. Here the student has to perform on a modest scale the operation of criticism. Two sets of data are at his disposal; one is particular, and made up of the thousand and one intimations of the author's purport and mood, into which his utterance, once properly scrutinized and fully lived through, is resolved. The other is more general, and comprises the total knowledge and impression of the writer's personality, which has previously been gathered from reading and study, together with the very significance of the passage in hand, not as a complex of individual meanings, but as a living expression of a mental life. Those two sets of elements are originally distinct, but hardly remain so; the synthesis is effected in flashes; like goes to like, affinities find each other out, and the mood of the passage is illuminated by being fused with the mental organization out of which it grew, and a part of which it remains. This intuitive perception of the why and the wherefore of a text is thus nothing else but the realization of the intimate necessary dependence which links it up with the being, thought and art of a writer. As in criticism properly so called, we have here the reading of the development which has produced the expression of a mind, and so an interpretation of that mind itself; but the scope in the present instance is not so wide, the object being limited; that psychological interpretation, instead of being sought for its own sake, is called in only as a means to an end, which is and remains the elucidation of a single passage. A satisfactory *explication de texte* should not grow out of bounds, and aim at setting up the full-length portrait of an author; it should rather, from the brief but suggestive evocation of a personality, latent in a given utterance, derive the light that is just needed to illuminate the utterance itself. If it rises from the particular to the general, it returns at once, with a firmer assurance, to the particular problem from which it started.

The power upon which the whole operation revolves, is the magnetism which attracts to one another the fit elements of the synthesis that is preparing. That force, though elusive, is not exactly mysterious; it grows with the growth of certain faculties, and it is fed by certain experiences and labors of the mind; indirectly at least, we can thus catch a glimpse of its nature. It is mainly the subtle sense of affinities; and although the field of its exercise is here that of art, those affinities in themselves are not so much æsthetic as psychological. What makes a student able to practice successfully that explanation of an isolated passage in the light of the original creative temperament which impregnates it, is his being gifted with the intuitive divination of personality: an instinct that enters easily and swiftly into the laws of mutual dependence, by which mental traits and characteristics are bound together, and which govern their organization into possible wholes. Now the art of life consists mainly in reading character, and interpreting the conditions of things; a shrewd instinct of possibilities and congruity is at the root of common sense; and moral judgment itself is largely governed by that delicate appreciation of fine shades. We are led to realize that a training in critical interpretation, thus understood, does impart to higher literary studies the value of a spiritual culture, and is conducive to a more interior knowledge of man.

Those remarks may well seem to have deflected the course of our inquiry from the ground where we had chosen to place, and tried to maintain it: the most ordinary unpretending level of acquaintance with literature, as pursued by the common run of students. But while the process under dissection looked perhaps somewhat strained, the process in being is plain, normal and reassuring enough. The *explication de texte* is done every day by quiet, average young men and women, though it attracts of course the more brilliant, and can then become a labor of love, performed with enthusiasm; it is not necessarily a schooling for intended critics or men of letters; it is simply an exercise for the development of psychological insight, as the best, the only means to acquire literary perception. In that modest routine, with no wordy pretentiousness, and a good deal of academic caution, the faculty of valid criticism—valid because sincere—which is latent in every mind, can best be stimulated and encouraged; no more should be needed to recommend it.

May the future spare us the plague of a pan-critical age, with a Babel of shrill individualities aggressively expressing themselves. But the desire and the power of seeing and feeling for oneself the grounds of one's literary likes and dislikes, and of interpreting books in terms of intellectual life, might be conceded to all partakers in a civilization which lays stress on the full development of every being. And should that addition to the usual routine of higher studies contribute to humanize somewhat the present atmosphere of literary departments, there might be a majority among our American colleagues and friends to think that it was not, when all was considered, a change for the worse.

THE METHOD OF DISCONTINUITY IN MODERN ART AND LITERATURE

THE METHOD OF DISCONTINUITY IN MODERN ART AND LITERATURE [1]

New and "advanced" art is proverbially difficult. The initiated worshipper of the latest cult takes pride in tasting austere joys, which baffle the attempts of the Philistine. Novelty is more easily achieved in form than in thought; and as art cannot thrive unless its appeal is refreshed at intervals, we are used to expect that revolutions in style will take place now and again. Fashions come and go, and reappear, in other things than hats and dresses. No wonder, then, that within each mode of artistic expression, new generations should set their hearts on an avoidance of traditional form.

If we survey the whole field and course of a given civilization, the differences between the developments of the various arts will tend to vanish; and they will fall into fairly well defined periods, in each of which some one characteristic will assume a prominent value. Again, for some time, the culture of the world has grown more and more unified; and æsthetic fashions at the present day are to a large extent international.

When considering the achievements of the last

[1] May, 1924.

forty or fifty years in Europe and America, one of the features that strikes our attention most is the parallel emergence, in all the arts, of a movement away from a need which, whether in the ascendant or not, was always felt and honored: the craving for some sort of continuity in form.

Among the various periodical changes in the progress of art, that which most naturally takes place, because it answers a chronic desire of the human mind most easily, is the change from the simple to the complex. The forms that suited our fathers because they were just irregular enough to be pleasant, are apt to grow most flatly stale and over-symmetrical to us. Thus regularity of structure is the most relative of æsthetic values; no other undergoes variation of quite the same magnitude. Now it is a fact at the present day, and has been for some time, that in its effort to renew itself, art has significantly laid stress on that particular element in the condition of regularity, which appears as an unbroken, continuous tenor of expression; the stress being a decidedly negative one. A discontinuous mode of presentment has been sought by an increasing number of artists; and the craving for discontinuity has very generally moved towards a climax, which in some arts may have been reached, whilst in others it may not have been yet.

Painting first showed a decided breaking from an ideal which seemed an inseparable part of its very aim and purpose. Well before the end of the nineteenth century, impressionism had won a place for itself in all the leading countries; and its influence was soon felt on the technique of all painters. Color asserted its full rights at the expense of drawing; objects lost the complete, rounded outlines which were thought to be part and parcel of their identities; and the synthetic tone-impressions were produced by disconnected color stains. How "pointillism" evolved out of impressionism, is matter of common knowledge. Pictures got more and more discontinuous, and a line long enough to be measured became the unpardonable sin, until the reaction came, and "cubism" reasserted the virtues of line and pattern with a vengeance. But the cubists have failed to carry the art with them; and in so far as one can speak of a common standard of painting, it remains at the present day largely swayed by the methods of impressionism.

The turn of music came next. For centuries, each new genius had been hailed as a law-breaker, a dull-eared fierce barbarian, playing havoc with melody; until his bold departures from the traditional patterns grew familiar, and tradition began to cling to them. Mozart's discords had raised a storm, and so had Beethoven's; then Wagner came, who broke musical expression into units, and recomposed those units into the richest symphonic developments. After much grumbling, he was at last swallowed; and feeling sure that this time the limit had been reached, the man in the street settled down comfortably to a quiet enjoyment of the fashionable concerts. Little did he expect what was in store for him. The last generation has extended the bounds of tolerable discords beyond the dreams of thirty years ago; and melody, whilst it will unexpectedly revive here and there, is mostly, in its older sense, a thing of the past; it has, at least, ceased to organize itself at once upon the blank of the average listener's attention, into a pretty symmetrical pattern of sounds. The unity in diversity which musical beauty requires, shows us now a very marked predominance of diversity; and discontinuous schemes, as well as discontinuous sounds, are almost the rule.

A similar change may, to a large extent, be traced in sculpture, the decisive influence in recent developments being probably that of Rodin, as it was Debussy's in the field of music. The tangible shapes of human bodies are no longer limited by rounded finished outlines; everything is made subservient, not to the sense of touch, but to that of sight; and the solid impression of the eyes is suggested, not given ready-made, by a complex interworking of harsh, vigorous, incomplete contours. Lines are not done away with altogether; but they are decidedly discontinuous, as are surfaces. One might possibly follow up the analogy through architecture; and note the part played by a systematic violation of symmetry, as well as the rarity of uninterrupted outlines, both in ambitious monuments, and the more humble dwelling-houses. But this art is least governed by inner, psychological processes; material changes, practical inventions, social happenings, are the main forces in its evolution; and that evolution is broken into a confusing mass of secondary movements.

Literature allowed some of the other arts to get the start of it at first; but it then more than made up for lost time; and it is now second to none in the enthusiasm with which it has taken up the new tendency. Dealing with letters, we come to a field in which periods are perhaps more clearly defined, and more naturally connected with the general progress of thought. We thus find it easier to trace the advance of the fashion, and to bring it back to deeply-lying causes in the psychological development of the times. It is possible to say that the last well-marked period through which European letters have been going, was a new romanticism, which gained the ascendancy between 1875 and 1890, and had not yet run its full course when the Great War broke out. The fortune of the discontinuous mode of writing is inseparable from that wave of romantic inspiration.

The romanticism of 1800-1830 had been a revolt against the conventional cut-and-dried classical patterns, in the manner as well as the matter. To the orthodox reviewer of 1816, Coleridge's *Ancient Mariner* or Shelley's *Alastor* suffered from a feverish, morbid intensity of mood, which not only destroyed the fine balance and lucid aptness without which no poetry could be sane, but shattered the smooth tenor of elegant expression. Coleridge's poem seemed rough and jerky; Shelleys' invertebrate and sprawling. In those writers, and in their most eminent contemporaries, the architecture and continuity of thought and phrasing were obviously the worse for what was, to all appearances, the unbalanced enthusiasm of literary zealots. And yet, strange to say, it was well before the romantic age that a writer who was only in some respects a forerunner of it, had reached at one stroke what remained for a century the climax of discontinuity. Sterne's *Tristram Shandy* sought for humorous effects in nothing more persistently than in broken, disconnected, incomplete statements.

The Victorian Age in England, and the corresponding period in France, tied the knot of a well-knit style with a firmer hand. The stress was laid again on artistic finish; with the majority of writers, reason, science, objectivity, were the watchwords; and a solid frame of ideas, or a body of conscious æsthetic scruples, made the work of art a constructed thing. An exception in his own time, a prophet and pourer of the vials of wrath, Carlyle stood out, with his fiery ardor and impatient, irregular speech, cut into twisted, disjointed fragments.

Victorian self-satisfaction had hardly begun to be shaken by the doubts, anxieties, curiosities, and dreams of the new romanticism, when literature started on the course which was to bring it to the extreme discontinuity of recent years. Meredith made his heroes think aloud, or thought for them; and their thought, like his own, was a series of flashes, with which a half-impressionist style made shift to keep up. In France, the symbolist school denounced the rhetoric and stiff majesty of the Parnasse; Verlaine brought poetry down to the poignant, spontaneous, loosely constructed language of a child; Mallarmé loaded it with subtle, mysterious symbols, and his syntax was no less original and difficult than his wording. Then the "décadents" came, and for a while obscurity was the rule in an esoteric literature, in which the connection between terms and thoughts was a matter of mood or fancy, instead of argument and logic. At the same time, the mold of the traditional French verse, which the romanticists had broadened without breaking it, was decidedly cast aside; and the "vers libre" poets tried to destroy an element of regularity in measure and cadence, which was essential to the perception of continuity in verse.

Meanwhile English letters were following suit, through the "yellow nineties," and after; they had their own impressionism, symbolism, decadentism. In prose as well as in poetry a greater freedom of expression answered to the outspokenness of the age. Yet, whilst using that freedom, the normal English writer respected the normal structure of the English sentence. With all its explosive, brusque vigor, Kipling's style had not only sinews but a backbone. It was with a few writers, and in tentative pieces, that expression tended to be merged into a series of jottings, the only unity of which was in their common power of suggestion. Indeed the literature of discontinuity was never popular; it hardly spread beyond the fringes of refined, intellectual circles. But from the time when D. G. Rossetti wrote his last poems, and Meredith his latest novels and lyrics, there had been in English letters a distinct vein of expression, in which the complexity or searchingness of thought told on the accustomed texture of speech, and often made the regular sequence of words subservient to original effects. In France, for the last thirty years, this vein has been broader than in England, and the more remarkable for its contrast with the usual clarity and symmetry of the French language.

The last fifteen years have brought the tendency to a head. Whilst, on the one hand, the second romantic tide is at slack water or has begun to ebb, the principle of discontinuity in words, on the other hand, has been carried to unparalleled lengths. France has her classical reaction; England shows some symptoms of having hers; Georgian poetry has rather swung back to definiteness of mood and verse. Still, many eminent writers in France, some of them numbered among the classicists, and many less eminent, are more than ever relying on discontinuous presentment. The prose of Marcel Proust, amorphous and indefinite, endlessly wound its tortuous way through the intricacies of character. The "surréalistes" have adopted a style in which words are just impressionist color stains, and are dumped down on the page, without the slightest regard for syntax, in groups governed only by experience or affinity. The language of the Goncourts, of Claudel, of Francis Jammes, of Paul Fort, to mention widely different shades of freedom, was nothing to this. In England and America, several of the most original writers are rivalling the boldest discontinuity of the musicians or painters. In this school, Mr. Ezra Pound, Mrs. Virginia Woolf, hold distinguished ranks; but the Mr. Joyce of *Ulysses* should bear the bell. Moreover, it is easy to see that a good deal of the most up-to-date dramatic production, in all countries, is impelled along the same lines by the combined influences of Russian art, and of the moving pictures; and German "expressionism," in its confused wealth of tendencies, cherished a fondness for the spontaneous, uncoördinated vision and language of the mind. Lastly, it may be more than a mere coincidence, that the "quantum" theory should have set the minds of the physicists, of late, working and wondering on the paradoxical discontinuity that tends to be substituted for the transmission of energy on the unbroken rhythm of wave-lengths.

Those remarkably widespread and intense symptoms should be accounted for by something more than the persistent spirit of the neo-romantic age. That this spirit was responsible for the beginnings and early advance of the modern discontinuous craze, can hardly be doubted. No less efficiently about the end than at the beginning of the nineteenth century, romanticism had promoted a rebellion of the emotional being; it had denied the discipline of the intellect. Its energy was fed by an eruption of the subconscious; in a direct contact with the realities of the inner life lay its strength; upon that, and nothing else, it took its stand. No more natural consequence could ensue than the romantic eagerness for a concrete, a complete, an unadulterated expression of the self. Immediacy of presentment was an inevitable enemy to construction. The elementary, passionate elements of the soul gave birth to utterances that would tend to be disconnected and uneven, as is the rhythm of emotion itself.

It is one of the paradoxes of the present time, that with those desires, very different motives should combine, so as to produce the extreme attempts which the school of discontinuity have recently made. On top of the romantic wave, and carried onward by it, the "new psychology" has burst upon the world; and as it measures the climax of a phase of thought, it is probably the vanguard of the coming and inevitable reaction. In it the sense of intuitive values is turned into an instrument for intellectual, analytical knowledge; at the core of the new science lies the objective desire for truth. By its very nature, the latter movement is thus substantially opposed to the former. In spite of largely converging literary effects, this inner discrepancy should be emphasized.

It sheds additional light on the fact, otherwise apparent enough, that whilst being the extreme offshoots of the romantic spirit, the recent discontinuous writers are the symptoms of a transition.

The advance of psychology during the last thirty years has resulted in the spread of a totally different notion of the inner world. Psycho-analysis, with its insistence on the subconscious, repressions, and the ever-present action of sexuality, is only a secondary aspect of that advance. What chiefly matters is that to the disciples of James and Bergson, the system of intellectualized diagrams which used to be taken for an exact mapping out of the mind, was no longer tenable. From those philosophers the reading public gradually received a much more concrete impression of the strange, shifting, incalculable realities of the consciousness. The mechanism of the utilitarians, and the logic of the metaphysicians, gave place to a method of subtle, vivid perception and intuition. The unity and continuity of thought, which had been taken for granted, were thus found to be largely an illusion, worked out by the imperious needs of the human intellect. Whilst the stuff of consciousness was in a way homogeneous, and its elements influenced and interpenetrated one another, it could no longer be systematized and constructed easily from the outside. To all practical purposes, the new view of the mind was that of an extremely complex and discontinuous mass of ever original states, which somehow felt itself one, but at the same time felt itself whole in each of its numberless fragments, and was anything but simple to the eyes of the onlooker.

That revolutionized view of what remains the central subject to most writers, the mind of man, is the deeper origin of an increasingly fertile literary motive, psychological realism. This grew to be, with some artists, the strongest incentive to creation; and we need not seek anywhere else for the cause of the extreme lengths to which the method of discontinuity has been recently carried.

The truth of the soul, the whole truth, and nothing but the truth: such is the scientific ideal which has again possessed many novelists. Whether analytical or intuitive, their knowledge of the inner world must be given direct expression. Form, with the diagrams, constructions, conventions that clung to it and were hardly separable from it, was a veil between the creative impulse and the reader's mind. So form, or stereotyped habits of expression, were to be entirely done away with. Renunciation to it in every mode—as order, symmetry, pattern, traditional style, or even syntax—became a desirable end in itself. To an æsthetic conscience pitched in that key, a more direct revelation of the artist's mood does not only result in truer art; it produces, or should produce, a heightened pleasure.

Those motives have entered into some of the discontinuous effects sought by contemporary musicians and painters. But they have been chiefly active in that art which deals most fully and minutely, if not perhaps most directly, with the human mind as its object: literature. They underlie the superficially divergent aims of the masters of the new technique. To study this, the most appropriate example might be the typical case of Mr. Joyce.

Whatever judgment one may pass on *Ulysses,* that work deserves attention as an uncompromising attempt to dispense with the traditional methods of construction. It is obvious that the author does not want his book to be merely chaotic; and he is clearly at some pains to sink into the very substance of his material the elements and the means of a more subtle organization. Of his success in that particular endeavor, different views may be maintained. But there can be only one opinion as to the efficiency of his effort to write disconnectedly. We find at least no apparent coherence or transition between most of the various parts; the text is usually made up of mere jottings, which represent the spontaneous succession of images in the consciousness of the heroes; no material distinction is made between the silent, inner language of the mind to itself, and its spoken words to others; unchecked play is given to the laws of contiguity and resemblance, which govern our associations of ideas, and no other unity is sought than that of the actual course of our day-dreams; stripped to essentials, the average sentence bears no relation whatever to the habits of literary style and the grammatical rules of the structure or se-

quence of clauses; whilst punctuation, practically restricted to the most common signs in the body of
the book, is completely absent from the last forty
pages. Indeed, no more remarkable example could
be quoted of the uses to which the new principle has
been put by literature. The fortune of the "inner
monologue," in all countries and all languages, tes-
tifies to the very general existence of a frame of
mind which finds its most natural outlet in that
mode of expression.

Having briefly followed the method of discontinuity through the traditional æsthetic provinces, we
come next to the recent popular art which seems to
have sprung from that very method as its central
root. What made the moving pictures possible was
at first a practical invention, a technical progress.
But the cinema palaces once opened, psychological
causes did most to further their tremendous success.
They answered to the natural tastes of normal men
and women, without the training and refinement of
higher culture. They offered the realism of every-
day life, the documentary picturesqueness of snap-
shot views; and they very soon were brought to
offer scenes of easy humor, cheap drama and sentiment. On the other hand, whilst they gave a surfeit
of images, they reduced the mental strain of the
spectator to a minimum. The construction of the
whole series or of each episode was of the simplest;
transitions were unnecessary; and the understood
connections needed to gather the plot were given

ready-made on the screen. The enjoyment of the show required only a mood of passiveness; and to such moderate demands, the many were eager to respond. It is undeniable that no recent social development has more broadly influenced the common mind; nor more specifically encouraged the preference of the natural Adam for a type of fiction at least as loosely knit as current experience. The desire for a certain kind of objective truth, and the dislike for a certain constructive intellectual exertion, were satisfied at the same time. It cannot thus be doubted that the universal favor of the picture palaces has contributed some of its elements to the atmosphere in which the principle of literary discontinuity has been able to thrive; just as the optics of the cinema have been responsible for some of the most recent developments in dramatic technique.

Before we try to pass judgment on the claims of discontinuity in themselves, and on their results, it may not be amiss to point out that this principle is not in any way self-sufficient and final. It is a method, a means to an end; and that end is so entirely distinct and separate, that it can be formulated in just the contrary terms. The object of the method is directly to create truth, indirectly pleasure; and that truth is a vision of the world under the aspect of *continuity*. The elaborate oppositions and differences created by the intellect are ignored, evaded, weakened; the broken, interrupted mass of images, sensations, and elementary units of thought, merges into one tenor and one homogeneous sequence. Indiscrimination is the outcome of extreme and haphazard discrimination. The universe of Mr. Joyce is a pantheistic dream in which nature and the soul are one and equally indefinite. The spell of discontinuous art, in music, painting, the drama, and writings of all kinds, works upon us like a hallucination; the intelligence, always exacting and diffident, is set at rest; our senses and imaginations are drowned in the soft-whirling, rippling current of things. A trance seizes our minds and our wills. The audiences in picture palaces know that hypnotic effect well, and are very probably fond of it.

What, then, are the merits and can be the future of discontinuity? As put to practice in recent attempts, it has probably reached the limit that, with the utmost stretch of elasticity, a sane taste could be brought to accept. Even so, it has served a purpose, and been a very useful æsthetic experiment. Taken as a whole, it has justified itself in its artistic consequences. It was, to begin with, an inevitable reaction; the constructive faculties had been indulged to an excess; philosophy, science, and art, were equally the better for a change which broke through the crust of schemes and concepts, to the living realities below. The discontinuous method is certainly truer to fact than was the naïvely continuous tradition of the past. The perception of this truth can be agreeable; and in so far as the reduction of complexity to unity is a pleasure, the new art is not only more complex and more fresh, but more efficient.

It must be confessed, however, that art cannot live without some sort of perceptible organization; and that all is not well when an organic unity is to be established by the reader, listener or spectator, at the cost of a very strenuous effort. Pleasurable feelings are apt to vanish under the strain; and some temperaments may bear it longer than others, but a time comes for all when the most heroic stubbornness must confess itself beaten. At that stage, we say that the work lacks order, architecture, balance, to the extent of losing the elusive virtue of beauty. Now, the latest expressions of the discontinuous principle, in all fields, have come dangerously close to that limit, or passed it. A reaction has begun in painting; it may not be far in music; whilst in literature, some symptoms are already betraying its approach. It is not perhaps unfair to Mr. Joyce to say that the hard-won and still disputed success of *Ulysses* will not so much open the way to new works of the same kind, as bring together the gathering forces of a revolt against the extremities of formlessness in art.

According to precedents, the present years of transition should lead us to a new age of rationality, equilibrium, and order—a classical age. A movement in that direction has grown to be the predominant influence in French letters; it is not improbable that on different lines, the literatures of other countries should show a parallel change. Though the cubists have not won the day, they are leaving a mark on painters; and in the conflict of pictorial tendencies, a synthesis is maturing which will no doubt reëstablish to some extent the rights of form. Music is feeling her way to some extremely broad elastic law, which should reconcile the absolute freedom of the artist with a modicum of harmony. The same is likely to be the characteristic feature of the synthetic period which after-war literature is to all appearances entering. Still, the constructive inspiration and style that reassert themselves will leave a wider margin for the discontinuous effects, which have finally found a place among the legitimate resources of art.

PSYCHO-ANALYSIS AND LITERARY CRITICISM

PSYCHO-ANALYSIS AND LITERARY CRITICISM

I

Psycho-analysis is still very much in the air at present.[1] The flood of explanation, discussion, and comment shows no decrease; and whilst the learned disagree as to the merits of the new method, the common man, and the man of letters, have eagerly seized upon its sensational or dramatic possibilities. Having spread rapidly over Europe, and from the Old World to the New, it has entered into the very consciousness of our time.

A working knowledge of it can thus be taken for granted. Still, it may not be entirely superfluous to repeat that psycho-analysis, with which the name of Freud, and perhaps that of Jung, are prominently associated, is before all an analysis of the "psyche," or of the whole soul, not excluding the subconscious self. This is normally hidden and repressed; it expresses itself through dreams, and is secretly at work in the higher activities of the mind. Unravelling the tangled threads of inner experience, the "complexes" or abnormalities of character, and the elusive logic of dream states, the specialist can probe the mysteries of the subconscious. What he discovers is a

[1] May, 1924.

sort of obscured and buried layer, the confused mass of pre-human or barbarous development; a pitiless, brutal or shameful domain, lying under the clear world of civilized, moralized being. In that region of ourselves, instinct is a supreme law; and all instincts are more or less directly connected with the "libido" or desire of the sentient being for the satisfaction of its appetites. Among the various forms of the libido, the sexual are practically predominant. Following those clues through the puzzles of behavior and the riddles of artistic expression, turning to use the involuntary confessions to be found in the visions of the dreamer, the imaginings of the poet, and all the spontaneous initiatives of the soul, the mental doctor can effect cures; he throws a ray of light on the hidden cause; and by revealing to us our secret wishes, enables us to satisfy or to eradicate them.

It can be seen from this extremely brief account that psycho-analysis has no less to do with the problem of art than with that of morality. The object of the following short study is not to pass judgment once more on the merit of the doctrine: that should be left to the competent persons; nor even to examine its relation to creative literature, a field in which it has been, for better for worse, a strongly stimulating influence. The "new psychology," as it is loosely called, to-day plays the part of that latest addition to the body of accessible scientific theories, which is in the modern world, to the imaginations of writers, what the leading religious or social belief was to those of previous centuries. If, as was expected by the philosophers, general ideas have succeeded dogma in the intellectual direction of mankind, the ideas that really assume power are not those of the metaphysician, for very obvious reasons. Even the physics of Einstein finds few imaginative renderings, for reasons no less obvious. But the teaching of Freud has awakened an immediate and a universal echo. Perhaps the reasons, here again, are not far to seek. Leaving out the abundant literature which—be it novels, or poetry, or drama—is instinct with psycho-analytical curiosities or enthusiasm, my purpose is only to try and seek what auxiliary help the new lore has brought or can bring to literary criticism.

The relation between these two terms is natural, and has been promptly emphasized. The critic is an analyst in his way; a book is originally, and remains before all, an organization of psychological elements. There is a very apparent analogy between imaginative productions and dreams; an analogy which æsthetics have long felt. The latest development of modern criticism, its return to an impressionistic ideal, which it attempts to deepen through a stimulation of artistic consciousness, and on the other hand the whole course of recent psychology towards a fuller realization of the spontaneous and subconscious activities, are movements on converging lines.

If we survey the applications thus far made of psycho-analysis to the criticism of literature, we find that they can be divided into two groups of unequal size, according as their object is general or particular. In the former and smaller group may be mentioned Professor Prescott's *The Poetic Mind,* and the first part of Mr. Mordell's *The Erotic Motive in Literature.* As examples of the latter we might quote the various literary cases examined in Freud's own works; Mr. Ernest Jones's famous interpretation of *Hamlet;* the second part of Mr. Mordell's study, previously cited; and Mr. Collins's *The Doctor Looks at Literature.*[1] It seems to me that criticism can derive substantial benefit from the general methods of psycho-analysis, and that the problems of interpretation cannot ignore that new way of approach. I believe, on the other hand, that most of the attempts made, on dogmatic psycho-analytical lines, to solve the individual riddles of literature, and deal with artistic personalities, leave us in the mood of dissatisfaction and revolt. Such are the conclusions which it will be the modest endeavor of a layman to establish.

They imply some sort of a reaction to the claims of psycho-analysis itself; and though the proper valuation of those claims belongs only to the professional philosopher, it would be futile to pretend that

[1] F. C. Prescott, *The Poetic Mind,* 1922; A. Mordell, *The Erotic Motive in Literature,* 1919; Ernest Jones, *Essays in Applied Psycho-Analysis,* 1923; J. Collins, *The Doctor Looks at Literature,* 1923.

I am not here trespassing upon his domain. So I had better give myself away at once.

In the light of simple common sense, psycho-analysis cannot be dismissed with a shrug of the shoulders, or a flat refusal to take it seriously. However glaring its exaggerations and faults, it has come to stay. The modern mind has grown aware of an "other side" to our inner life; in some form, the subconscious will play its part in the knowledge and the ethics of man. One glance over the trend of thought since the Renaissance will show us that new and still newer layers of our deeper beings have been gradually laid bare. Romanticism was the outstanding event in that process of self-realization; but that irresistible surge of the long repressed emotions has not been the only means of their late recognition by an over-intellectualized world; even among the intellectualists, and through the rational centuries, men of stronger insight had been at work, deciphering the hidden play of instincts. In England only, the first Samuel Butler, whom the second was to echo so strangely, then Swift and Mandeville, had dug up unexpected ore from their cynical burrowings; Hazlitt, and the Thackeray of *Vanity Fair,* followed after them. The exploration of the human mind, during the last fifty years, has chiefly busied itself with the origins and roots of things. The novel had taken that turn, before Freud came and recommended it to the novelists. The "new psychology" is a complement and consecration which the trained searchers have added to the intuitions and discoveries of the men of letters.

In so far as it is a necessary product of our time, and brings to a head latent elements or prevailing tendencies, psycho-analysis will probably stand its ground. But we cannot feel the same confidence as to any of its original theories and pet formulæ. The vigorous, dogmatic twist it tries to give to our notion of the subconscious life, meets not only with the opposition of many specialists, but with a resistance no less stubborn in most men's intuitive sense of reality. Even such of us as allow their fancy to play with the universal, all-embracing empire of the "libido" know that, to all practical purposes, there is no such thing. The dissections of infantile love, and the awful "Œdipus complex," leave us utterly unconvinced. Freud's interpretations of dreams are no less unreal than they are clever. We feel all along that such constructions can be put, after the event, upon almost everything. Indeed, psycho-analysis may be a magic key to open the secret chambers of the heart; but the only genuine discoveries it has so far made are not properly its own; and as we shall see, the key possesses no sure, unfailing virtue in itself; it is to be laboriously adapted to each lock. In that adaptation—in the attentive study of all the special elements of each case—the value of the process lies. Now that is exactly what we might expect from the old biographical method of approach, completed and enlarged by a sane assimilation of the

most solid results of common present-day psychology.

II

Professor Prescott's study of the *poetic mind* is
a very interesting attempt to turn upon his subject
the general light derived from the broadest notions
and central endeavor of psycho-analysis. A theory
of poetry bold and original, though encouraged and
guided by many previous attempts, is thus connected,
at a vital point, with the most acceptable elements
in the doctrine of Freud.

There is much in common between that still mysterious activity, the invention of poets, and the spontaneous exercise of the imagination, either in day-
dreaming, or in the dreams of night. Our mind is
then liberated from the yoke of its normally practical and purposive thought; free play is granted to
the mutual affinities of images; they associate of
themselves, in groups whose peculiar logic or rather
habits (contiguity, resemblances, etc.) have been
summarily traced. There is a resilience, an energy,
in that power of relatively unlimited development;
it is the psychological reality of "inspirations." An
indefinite possibility of forming new associations:
such is the expansive force which is at the root of
the "poetic" feeling.

Now, it is a well-known fact that in all such
frames of mind, when the will and the intellect have
abdicated, the emotions step into their places, and

carry on. Whether we are awake or sleep, they play a predominant part in guiding the free associations of images. Here it is, then, that psycho-analysis comes in. The subconscious, most often the repressed desires of the self, are thus brought into direct contact with poetic invention. They are normally the fountain-head of its capricious course.

Professor Prescott's thesis should not be judged apart from the many illustrations and confirmations which he is able to bring forth. For our present purpose, it will be sufficient to sum up one main objection, and the answer. Exception may be taken to such a view of poetry, which seems to do away altogether with the intellectual element of inspiration. A long poem has to be planned out. Measure and proportion are to be established between the various themes. Some sort of logical sequence must be followed out. Ideas, not rarely to a high degree abstract and subtle, must be expressed. There is a philosophy at the back of all poetry; and even where it is not materially apparent, its presence and magnetism are felt. All that is true; but construction, thinking, and the labor of careful expression, belong to the artistic, not to the properly poetical part of the æsthetic task. The poets who have deliberately thought out all their effects, and assigned each its relative value, may be very distinguished writers of verse; they miss the something which is the supreme grace, and indeed the essence of poetry.

Other chapters of literary criticism can be illuminated in the same way, by side-lights from some of the main doctrines of psycho-analysis. However skeptical Freud's studies of particular dreams may leave us, he has done useful work in finding names for the tricks which the subconscious genius of dreams spontaneously develops, under the stress of repression and the "censorship." Professor Prescott turns "condensation" to clever use as a fit formula for one of the principal methods in the creation of fictitious characters; "displacement" as a general mode, under which all the manners of indirect presentment or suggestion are implicated. Symbolic expression is thus brought into touch with the natural working of the free imagination; and the inherent symbolism of all poetry duly emphasized.

The least felicitous part of this brilliant study is probably that in which the author tries to go beyond the stage of general psychological derivation; where he gives diagrams of the subconscious activities of the poetic mind, and attempts to reduce it to a somewhat mechanical precision. The working of substitution can hardly be represented with mathematical symbols, and assume the figure of an equation.[1] Some little gain in definiteness is thus purchased at too dear a price, and a dangerously false impression may be created in the reader. No two cases are alike in the history of the mind; no two associations identical. The relation of "á" to "a" is here an abstraction. The pursuit of a binding and ever-pres-

[1] *The Poetic Mind,* pp. 249-250.

ent connection between terms through such a process is vain. The psychological cause is related to the effect in such an elastic and peculiar manner that from a given effect, a given cause cannot be traced back with certainty.

III

That artificial hardening and stiffening of the elements of the mind is probably responsible for the repeated failures of the psycho-analysts, when they come to deal with individual problems, and insist on interpreting particular texts. Here they adopt the dogmatic and deductive method. Each special case is subordinated to ready-made outlines, and the rulings of Freud are given as final, with the absolute trust of disciples in a prophet.

Mr. Mordell's book, *The Erotic Motive in Literature,* deals first with generalities, and its conclusions are so far acceptable enough; but they do not add perceptibly to our knowledge. The practical points which psycho-analysis makes more triumphantly are those which had often been made before. To demonstrate at some length that the writer, not least when he prides himself on his objectivity, is always present in his work, does not take us beyond the familiar landmarks of ordinary criticism. We need hardly be reminded that love, in literature as in life, is very generally present and active. We knew that the self-expressions of writers abounded in "consolatory mechanisms"; had not Gœthe, for instance, found out a century and a half ago that the out-pouring of fictitious emotions into *Werther* was the best way to allay in his own soul the fever of real passion? How the characters of villains and traitors are created from the gentle personalities of play-wrights and novelists, and how a spiritual bond of filiation can unite a Shakespeare to the most various specimens of human nature, was no longer a mystery before Mr. Mordell wrote. To trace the almost uni-versal diffusion of morbidness in modern literature to the repression of amatory instincts in children, is at best only a half truth, and of that the roman-ticists had made us fully aware.

But even through those chapters we are startled by the unguarded confession of the most naïvely rigid determinism. Mr. Mordell finds it possible to affirm that the life of Dante being given, the *Divina Commedia,* with all the wealth of its unique char-acteristics, could be expected and was to follow as a necessary consequence. The psycho-analytic influ-ence in a writer's self, when found—and such dis-coveries, from the nature of the case, are most often conjectural—is turned into an all-sufficient and all-explaining cause. The problem of W. Cowper's more than half diseased mind had received pretty satis-factory solutions from a knowledge of his consti-tution, his temper, and the upsetting circumstances of his early career; but with those explanations the psycho-analyst disdains to have anything to do; the

Œdipus-complex is summoned, and at one stroke
the entangled knot of character and nerves is cut:
Cowper was passionately fond of his mother, and
the poem which he wrote "on receiving her portrait" is the key to his whole consciousness. A
bolder leap into the unknown is that through which
the critic takes us to the inmost core of Homer's
hazy, unsubstantial personality. The dream of
Achilles is the clearest self-revelation. The author of the *Iliad* here lets us into the secret of
his own master-emotion, a wounded and passionate
friendship. . . .

With its second part, the book more professedly
tackles individual problems; and the conclusion is
forced upon us, that whatever we can accept was
known to us before; whilst whatever is really new
we cannot accept. The romantic period, as was to
be expected, furnishes practically all the illustrations: the age of the great moral revolt was that
in which the deeper instincts rose to the higher regions of the soul, and the subconscious in man took
the direction of many lives. We are quite willing to
believe that Keats's love for Fanny Browne did lay
one of the most morbid strains in the rich tissue
of the *Odes;* but what profit is it to learn that the
Belle Dame sans Merci is an "anxious dream," with
all the orthodox Freudian marks of a disappointed
and inverted "libido"? And how are we to take
this most irritating pronouncement, that the poet's
wish to fly away with his nightingale into the volup-

tuous annihilation of death, is nothing but the expression of an erotic desire? It is in vain that Mr. Mordell quotes chapter and verse from the prophet of psycho-analysis; it leaves us unmoved to hear that according to Freud, all "flying dreams" have one and the same origin.

Worse, if possible, is to come. In the mood of Shelley's *Ode to the West Wind,* we are prepared to find the gathered and complex emotions of a poet's heart. It is a fact that Shelley, through the successive ardors of his most susceptible nature, was haunted, from the time of *Alastor,* by a bitter sense of the mutability of love.[1] But how could we bear with an attempt to show that the noble self-despair of the Ode—crossed, as it is, with the invincible surge of a final hope—is only the embittered and veiled utterance of a claim in favor of "polygamous instincts"? When he wishes to scatter, like dead leaves, "his thoughts among mankind," Shelley, we are told, is actuated by a repressed longing for the freedom of a wild, roaming love. . . . No wonder, next, that the lyric flight of the *Ode to a Skylark,* should be instinct, like Keats's *Nightingale,* with an "unconscious sexual symbolism."

Such astounding results should give us pause; and they may at least serve this end, to reveal in a condensed form the essential fallacy of psycho-analytical

[1] I have tried to interpret *Alastor* from a psycho-analytical point of view, in a somewhat fuller treatment of the theme of this lecture, *Revue de Littérature Comparée,* Juillet-Septembre 1924, pp. 467-471.

methods, when turned into an instrument for the dissection of personalities or texts. The error is one of exclusion and emphasis. That all the elements of consciousness are directly or indirectly interrelated, is a commonplace of psychology. All states of mind belong to an organic whole; and there is no part of that organism but enters into some sort of relation with all the others. Subtle links of resemblance, contiguity, or interpenetration can thus be found between thoughts, images, emotions, which actual experience has never brought together. Distant echoes of a psycho-physiological nature can be heard in the dim regions of the mind, uniting in an obscure harmony the muscular and emotional ecstasy of flying, imagined in the day-dreams of a poet, and his remembrances of the exaltation of love. There is nothing more in that organic connection than the fact of all-round interdependence, a fact which the universal reign of the so-called "sexual symbolism" well bears out. To magnify the relation into a significant and a causal one, to lend it a privileged value, and expect that it should make clearer the working of poetical genius, is confessing to a singular misconception of facts. Not only is the wealth of creative imagination and spiritual desire thus impoverished; but the æsthetic appreciation of art is entirely warped. Every mistake made in the interests of science is no doubt justifiable; but the literary critic who repeatedly labors under such a delusion shows himself gratuitously a prey to an obsession usually bred by the atmosphere of mental hospitals.

IV

Those vagaries, and similar ones—as, for instance, Mr. Ernest Jones's audacious interpretation of *Hamlet* in the light of the Œdipus-complex—can indeed be traced to an obsession; and this is in itself significant enough to justify a few remarks.

Doubtless sexuality is closely connected, in the more primitive regions of our nature, with all the entangled tendencies of man. There is no doubt as well that the higher activities of the mind spring from that same soil; and that the roots of moral enthusiasm or poetic inspiration are entwined with those of human love. There is no limit, either, to the possible affinities of psychological states. Passion, a localized focus in itself, radiates through our whole inner life. An inquiry upon our being which sets itself, as its special task, to follow up those more or less distant influences and relations, needs no excuse. Psycho-analysis was to have its chance; and it is natural that the critic should turn to it, for whatever help it can afford. That help has so far proved, in most concrete applications, rather disappointing, because the zeal of a necessitarian enthusiasm, and an over-simplified discipleship, are a dangerous mood in which to investigate the complex problems of the soul.

We can easily understand how the scientific devotion to truth should have assumed that half-fanatical garb. The whole nineteenth century gave itself doggedly to a pursuit of the primitive origins of things. Not only have the depths of the past been explored with a more keen and hopeful vigor; but in the present, the rich growths of civilization have been analyzed into the humbler elements which are still part and parcel of them. Democracy, the ethics of utility, the associationist psychology, and the philosophy of evolution, are various aspects of that levelling process. Psycho-analysis is to the study of the normal mind what Darwinism is to biology.

Below the superior domain of full consciousness does stretch the accumulated deposit of the untold development of the race. It is natural that in the experiences thus registered, the instincts and appetites of animality should reign practically unchecked. In calling our attention to the buried but still living roots from which the flowers of civilization and the life of the spirit have sprung, Freud and his school have enlarged our knowledge of ourselves. They have given the critic of art and literature a fuller intelligence of certain emotional reactions, cast a light on the spontaneous play of poetic fancy, and added a sharper edge to our appreciation of some effects. But modern man is before all what he is, what he wants to be, and is conscious of being. We are unjust to the soul that is always creating and molding itself, unless we reckon its aspirations among the most substantial realities. It is not enough, as the psycho-analysts do, to talk of "sub-limation." The primitive instincts which they discover within the highest ardors of the soul are not there present in the body, but like shrivelled blood-less ghosts; what is radiant with the fullness of life, what is essential, is the "sublimity" that the progress of the mind has evolved, and which constitutes a new order of being.

With this order of being æsthetic criticism has to do. Eagerly seized upon by over-enthusiastic disciples, the formula and phrases of psycho-analysis are dangerous, and no less in the interpretation of letters than in that of life. Their fault is not that they introduce an awkward complexity into our notion of the mind; but rather that they narrow and simplify it overmuch. What is one element among many, most often of negligible value, hardly ever predominant, is thus magnified into the all in all of motive, theme, and expression.

Sexuality is an important aspect of the subconscious; and the subconscious has its share in all the conscious activities. Whatever in art belongs chiefly to inspiration and invention cannot be studied apart from the subconscious. The critics and historians of literature must be prepared to find and gauge the influence of sexuality among the deepest forces which direct the artist in the choice of his subjects and his expressions. But in order to value properly the part played by that influence, it is indispensable that the critic should preserve an open mind, a delicate tact of the imagination and the heart, and a sense of proportion. Every case must be judged for itself; the spells and rules of a dogmatic witchcraft must be left severely alone, or used with the utmost caution. As a guiding light, the critic should keep before him the intuitive assurance of the freedom which, rising above the imperious instincts and suggestions of animality, endows the artist with a share of sovereign power, and makes his invention a queen in the sphere of images or words.

THE POSSIBILITIES OF THE NEAR FUTURE IN ENGLISH LETTERS

THE POSSIBILITIES OF THE NEAR FUTURE IN ENGLISH LETTERS [1]

Prophecy is a dangerous trade; and the reservations implied in the title of this lecture do not mend matters much. Still, stronger even than the spirit of scientific caution is our curiosity about the future; and there are cases when it may be wiser to indulge the wish than to repress it, provided we do not take ourselves, or our subject, too seriously. Indeed, an attempt like the present can only be excused on the score of its being a search, not for what will be, but for what is and has been; of its trying not to throw out oracular guesses, but to study from a new angle the ever present problem of artistic development.

That literature does not develop entirely at random, is here an indispensable assumption. It would be vain to follow up the lines of yesterday and today into those of a probable to-morrow, unless the latter were connected with the former by some relation of a more or less permanent nature. A degree of periodicity, a constant law in variation, must exist. Now such a law can be inferred from the course of the past; and a brief sketch of it should be given at once.

The web of literary history is woven of two min-

[1] May, 1924.

gling strains. One, the more essential, represents the contribution of the mind; the other, that of external and material circumstances. The former is a psychological tendency to the recurrence of two main moods, a period of predominant intellectuality being followed by a phase prevailingly imaginative and emotional, this in its turn calling for an era of intelligence, and so on. When that relatively regular order has been perceived in the history of a given literature—that of England for instance—we realize that the terms "classical" and "romantic" have, in common use, been detached from their originally narrow sense, and are practically the only words which we can employ to denote those two alternating literary tempers and ages. We grow aware, at the same time, that their succession allows of a wide margin of novelty and freshness, as the deeper memory of nations never forgets what they have actually lived through, and each new phase contains in itself the accumulated capital of previous experiences. In that way no moment of the present can be absolutely similar to any moment of the past, not even to those which it most closely resembles.

The other strain that enters into the shaping of literary history is the social evolution of the human group, whose collective mind finds expression in an original body of writings. The more important events and influences of an age, whether political or economic, have a direct bearing on the rhythm of psychological moods; according as they fall in with that rhythm, or rather run across it, they may give it a greater impetus, or check its course for a while; moreover, they always build the frame and historical figure of a period, thus offering to intellectual and artistic development the canvas on which it must paint itself.

In the light of that scheme, and leaving out the case of a sudden, totally unexpected disruption, such as a new world war, the possibilities of the near future in English letters can be to some extent conjectured from these known data of the present: first, the character of the last well-marked literary phase; then, the predominant influences in contemporary history.

It seems pretty safe to say that the last period which we can mark out and organize in the course of English, perhaps of European letters, was decidedly romantic. It began from 1875 to 1880, was in full swing between 1890 and 1910; slack water, or even the ebbing of the tide, was perceptible before 1914. There can be no doubt, again, that the Great War is the outstanding event whose shadow will stretch forward for some time yet. It is reasonable to expect that its influence will be felt decisively in the coming years, though that effect has not proved so immediate or simple as had been confidently announced. A new spiritual era has not dawned with the armistice. The earthquake did at first confuse all issues; it retarded the evolution of art, before it could quicken it.

The disappointment of the dark time which followed too sanguine hopes is upon us still. We dimly feel that a transition has begun; but whither it is taking us no one can say. Pessimism, in its turn, may be an ill-advised emotional reaction. That some precious seed has been sown into the harrowed soil of the modern world remains highly probable; but its growth might be slower than we had thought. In the domain of literature, the new inspiration will come with its full force not to the men who fought, but to their children. It is not war that is a second birth, but the recoil from it.

The inferences to be drawn from the recent course of events must thus be very guarded. But the facts of literary evolution during the last definite period, and at the present time, are a more solid ground to build upon. It is necessary that we should survey those facts before we can proceed any further.

The twentieth century in England has cut itself loose from the nineteenth. But in their revolt against the shibboleths of their fathers, the new generation did not take the time to be fair, and never troubled to draw nice distinctions. The decline of the Victorian spirit began before the long reign was over; and the break-up of that imperious tradition was not the work of a single day. The years from 1880 to 1914 have their unity in the more or less open defiance of the intellectual and social discipline which the preceding age had so triumphantly enforced. The stir of a renascent romanticism was then in the air. A more acute criticism shook the positive, simple faith in science which had given its religion to the mid-century. Philosophy labored with an idealist revival; the pendulum swung back from rationalism to pragmatism; a mystic note was heard again; Samuel Butler denounced the Darwinists and restated evolution in creative terms; George Meredith exalted the intelligence, but embodied its deepest teaching in the soul-felt lessons of Mother Earth. Meanwhile a decadent century was holding up orthodoxy to scorn; Swinburne and the symbolists in poetry, the naturalists and the æsthetes in art and morals, were rediscovering the romantic ardor, or following the freedom of the artist even to the self-imposed slavery of a passionate obedience. The quieter realism of a respectable age was being discarded in favor of the thrills of adventure and romance; the novel of imagination was born again. In the Celtic revival, the glow of yearning and the glamor of dreams were fed by the rekindled flame of national enthusiasm. Another revolt was that of the heart against the wrongs of the social order; from William Morris to Galsworthy, literature was instinct with the generous feeling of a bolder fraternity.

On the eve of the war, it looked as if the moral destruction had gone, in certain fields, far enough, or too far, for the silent genius which, in the dim regions of the subconscious, keeps watch over the destinies of races. Some signs seemed to show that the tide was turning, or setting again in the direction of a constructive ideal. Much of the prevailing romanticism still, but different tendencies as well, a desire to organize the emotions, the wills, and the doings of men around common beliefs of the character or of the mind, were to be found in the doctrines of action—the imperialism, the traditionalism, the socialism, of which Kipling, Chesterton, Wells, and Shaw were the prophets. Indeed, the psychological features of the period were anything but simple. As compared with any other age, the early twentieth century showed the greater complexity which its longer and more various heredity made only too natural. The subtle interplay of reason and instinct, of intelligence and intuition, in Shaw, Wells, and Galsworthy, no less than in Meredith and Butler, points to an intimate interpenetration of impulses, which qualifies the predominance of the leading motives, without destroying it.

If the preceding analysis has not been entirely mistaken, we should be able to expect, in the normal course of things, that the present transition should lead to one more constructive period, with a marked ascendancy of the intellectual or classical tendencies. The kindred values of order, balance, adjustment, finish, and rationality, would naturally be sought by the coming age, even though its very substance was permeated by the centrifugal desires and the inordinate longings of yesterday. No sooner has this possibility sketched itself out, than we become aware of what is at least a remarkable coincidence, though doubtless too perfect to turn out quite genuine in the end: the main legacy of the war so far has obviously been to create an immense desire for the readjustment of the world; and after the great havoc, the slogan of the last years has been the blessed word, reconstruction. Thus, at first sight, it would seem that in the literary phase which is probably beginning, the spontaneous rhythm of the mind, and the major historical influences, might not be at cross purposes, but confirm and strengthen one another.

No less striking is the analogy, that presses itself at once upon us, of the latest movement in French letters. A "classical" reaction had begun in France before the War; it has grown to be recognized as the leading feature of the present. Though it is far from drawing to itself all the talents, and though its political or social importance may be often exaggerated, there is no doubt that the most strenuous and systematic attempt to rally the widely divergent aspirations of the young writers round a common principle, has been made by the young "classicists." Their aims are obviously coherent, in so far as they stand at the same time for rational thinking, authority in government, and a constructive perfection of form in art. Now, the history of literature during the last hundred and twenty-five years shows us that new movements usually began in France and spread thence to England, especially when they were of an intellectualist nature, the most notable exception being the great romantic wave of the early nineteenth century, which crossed the Channel southward. We might then expect that the French classicists of the present day should be, in the flesh as well as the spirit, the harbingers of the literary school whose advent in England the logic of precedent leads us to foresee.

It is now time we should leave conjectures for realities, turn to Britain, and ask ourselves whether any visible symptoms there give support to our anticipations.

We can see at a glance that the present course of English letters offers us nothing at all comparable with the clear-cut doctrine and the partisan ardor of the French classicists. This in itself is no wonder: literary programs do not thrive on British soil; descriptions of aims in advance of realization are very infrequent, and schools are organized after the event by the judgment of the critics. A second glance shows us the greatest confusion of issues. Things are pretty much as they were before the war, with scattered tendencies, variously opposed temperaments, and few definite formulas. This, again, holds no surprise for us. The larger part of the literary output, in quantity, is always conservative, and shows no departure from the accepted types of yesterday. The vital movements—the seeds of the future—may remain for some time quite unnoticed.

It is natural, on the other hand, that the present moment should be remarkable for nothing more than for the divergence of its aims; never was the treasure of artistic tradition such a burden; never was the memory of the race so rich with dimly remembered images and rhythms, arrayed in all the successive fashions of the past. The increasing strain laid on the subconscious energies of the mind by the accumulated store of experience makes itself felt in the ever shorter duration of well-marked periods. A time has come when to all appearances the perception of a long series of æsthetic endeavors and successes is the dominant element of culture; that intimate knowledge, born in every sensibility that opens to art, gives each new voice the mellowness if innumerable half-forgotten echoes, but makes the absolute convincing originality of accents never heard before, an almost impossible gift. The question rises of itself, whether that eclectic old age in which the life of a national literature can be indefinitely and brilliantly prolonged, but does not allow of any decisive renewal, might not be beginning for some peoples of the old world, and particularly for France and England.

Taking stock of the whole field of English letters, we meet with a fair number of disconnected signs, substantial enough when brought together, and which might point to some progress towards a new period of the "classical" type. The typical men of this period, contrary to what is the case in France, would not claim a conscious kinship with the tradition of the classic centuries: whilst the nationalism of young French writers will turn to the age of Louis XIV for its æsthetic ideal, it is but exceptionally to the reign of Queen Anne and to Pope that the patriotic pride of English writers will turn. The word "classical" in England has no other spell than that with which it may have been invested by the ritual atmosphere of the schools and universities. But the name hardly matters. In its characteristics, the new phase would still possess the psychological substance of classicism, shot through, as is now the rule, with the attributes of the preceding, and of all phases.

Among the poets of recent years, a group apart might be formed of fastidious, scholarly writers, whose inspiration, in subject, manner, and language, harks back to the models of antiquity, or to the modern schools founded upon them. Lascelles Abercrombie, Sturge Moore, and J. Elroy Flecker, who died so young, do not properly belong to their own time, but to the continuity of an unbroken tradition. Again, the poetry of to-day is still, in its major aspects, fraught with a romantic spirit of freedom, unconstrained motion, and intuitive appeal; but close by daring attempts to break away definitively from the more or less regular pattern of measured verse, cadences are very often heard which testify to a refreshed and wiser preference of the ear for some sort of regular scheme in the music of the line. And

it must be acknowledged, that in the present-day
appreciation of values, the claims of the Restoration
and of the early eighteenth century are meeting with
a much more lively and ready acceptance. Whilst
the national sentiment still prefers the age of Eliza-
beth to that of Anne, not a few minds fondly choose
to dwell amid the graces and the manners of the
classical time of wit, lucidity and the couplet.

Criticism is in the present age, more truly than
it ever was before, a creative force, narrowly associated with the most spontaneous impulses of a
highly conscious time. It is a remarkable fact that
whilst the critics who have just passed away, Ra-
leigh, Clutton-Brock, relied mainly on the delicacy
of their sensitive insight, the most brilliant of the
younger men should use their penetration as a means
to a much more deliberate analysis. The method of
Lytton Strachey, Aldous Huxley, no less than their
style, bear the marks of French influence; their
works are intellectual to a degree rarely met with
in England.

Most of the critics of to-day dabble with psycho-
analysis; and many are the novelists, playwrights,
or poets who borrow from it the whole or part of
their inspiration. That current of ideas, complex as
it is, harmonizes readily enough with the symptoms
of a coming age of rationalism and lucidity. The
psycho-analyst lives on a stimulated subconscious-
ness, and thus takes his cue from the last romantic
revival. But his attitude is essentially unromantic. He

is out for self-knowledge, to the bitter end. His pas
sion is the scientific desire of the mind. His man
ner may be what he likes: there is at the back of i
the cold clear temper of the anatomist busy with a
knife. The very aim and the process of th
"new psychology" could not be reconciled with a
predominance of imaginative emotion; they belong
as of right, to the domain of the intellect. In so fa
as art is impregnated with them, it obeys the mag
netism of a new, or rather an old and a rejuvenated
ideal.

The same, or nearly, might be said of the extrem
lengths to which some prose writers and poets, in
various fields of literature, are pushing the method
of discontinuous presentment. As the hunger fo
truth was the guiding impulse of the psycho-analyst
these authors are swayed by the spirit of unflinch
ing objectivity. Their principle works out to a sys
tem of absolute jottings, free from every shred o
composition or sequence. They are thus in a direc
line the heirs of the preceding age, when the disci
plined kinds and patterns of the Victorian era wer
broken up by the rebellion of the intuitive forces
they only go one stage further on the road alread
marked out by the impressionist lyric or painting
free verse, the formless novel, etc. But it is easy t
see that by reaching, and passing, the limits com
patible with the average readers' assimilation of ar
tistic aims, they are opening the way for a reactio
in favor of coherence and logic. What is more ger

mane to our purpose is that they do bear in themselves the seeds of the rational age which is probably coming. Their mood is attuned to it in advance. Mr. Joyce's *Ulysses,* the short stories of Mrs. Virginia Woolf, are highly intellectual exercises. Their analytical ingenuity, and their bold endeavor to capture the elementary stuff of the inner life, are extremely interesting; but the range of their art is obviously limited by the lack of emotional appeal. Here again, we might say that the psychological substance of classicism is present, through the utter absence of classical and explicit construction. In the development of literature, such a paradox would naturally play the part of a transition.

More significant than those symptoms of actual movements, is the cast of thought that is spreading perceptibly, and bids fair to lend the next period its moral tone. For better for worse, the frame of mind into which the conflicting moods of the present seem to merge is one of decided, though somewhat embittered or despondent rationality. The ashy fruit of disillusionment, and the more sustaining harvest of human experience, are thus at one in nourishing a firm and patient resolve—the will to look things in the face, and square the hopes of the race with the iron laws of fate. The promise of a better world to come has not vanished, though it has receded into the distance. Now the worst of the after-war depression is over, the normal composure of the English mind seems to be in a process of recovery; the keynote of the near future rings out audibly: it is positive and experimental. The prevailing desire is for sanity. Those would be the features of an age of concentration and clear purpose, obviously fitted by its inner nature for the advent of one more "classical" period, in the broader sense which we submit that word should definitely assume.

Such are the omens of to-morrow, as we can read them. Those probabilities and possibilities are very far from making up a solid inference. Still, there may be enough in the thesis to render it worth arguing. However composite the next phase must and will be, it will, rather than not, bear that general stamp.

One might conceive, in the abstract, that the next phase should bear no recognizable stamp, because the capitalization of æsthetic moods threatens to destroy, in the long run, the law of psychological recurrence. The power of taking a fresh start has been perceptibly weakening; we have no perfect assurance that it is not on the eve of giving way. Should the era of stagnation draw near, classicism and romanticism would finally, in so far as England was concerned, be reconciled through eclecticism.

We are thus led to ask ourselves whether the moral and social conditions of the present encourage the hope that a fresh impulse might set loose new creative energy, and make it possible for the older nations of Europe to start again through the cycle of changes which they have almost covered to its final stage. Such a problem, wide as it is, could at least be fittingly taken up, as a conclusion to what must remain an ambitious argument.

There is no reason to believe that the genius of English literature has run its full course, and that its maturity, the marks even of a vigorous old age, must deprive it of the resilience which it showed in a glorious past. The history of every country bears witness to the elasticity of the spirit, to the happy perverseness of life; again and again, the foretold decay has turned out to be a new birth; the lie has been given to the laments of the prophets.

The Old World did expect to renew its youth in the ordeal of the war. That hope is much less sanguine now. But the nations of the West keep yearning for a fresh stimulus; and as they grope for it in earnest, they may find it. Many are the ways that could lead to the longed-for rejuvenescence. A return to nature has been the chronic desire of a sophisticated civilization. While Ruskin, and Morris, and Carpenter, seem to have failed, the essence of their teaching is slowly permeating an age better aware of the relation between physical and spiritual health. As England was the cradle of modern industry, hers is the race which has most clearly experienced its baneful effects. A future of garden-cities and open-air living would mean more than a purified blood: a cleansed soul. Then, the advent of labor to political authority may betoken the gradual development of a new social order; the rule of a more fully realized democracy would be more happy if it were more wise; in a nation of free guilds, culture, whatever its quality, would not be adulterated with the aristocratic legacy of the past; artistic impulses would rise more spontaneously from the native gifts of the people. Lastly, the dawn of an international organization throws a fresh, though perhaps a doubtful light, on the fate of the traditional literatures, with their exclusively national outlook. Can the cosmopolitan spirit that is bound to spread, infuse vitality into the intellectual life of human groups, whose strongest bond of union among themselves has been a feeling of separate kinship, as against the rest of the world? If the problem is susceptible of a positive solution, English literature will probably be one of those which thrive, instead of declining, on a more intimate and constant intercourse with the various families of man; it has already shown its assimilative energy; and the zeal with which the British people are taking up the cause of peace would point to some shifting of their ambition, from the field of imperialism on to that of moral influence among equals.

Those are the happy possibilities. Needless to say, others are to be considered, such as a new European war, or the opening of an era of social strife. There is something in the aspect of the world at present, as to the former risk, and as to the latter, in the character of the English people, which encourages us to take our stand on the side of optimism.

If there is an element of periodicity in the constant shifting of literary values, the coming decades of the twentieth century in England might see a rather strong body of achievements and efforts, aiming at an intellectual mastery of the mind over art and over form. This would not quench the ardor which must burn, whatever happens, in the imaginations of the sons, whether obedient or rebellious, of romanticism. But the shifting of the stress would be none the less perceptible.

PERIODICITY IN LITERATURE: THE FINAL STAGE

PERIODICITY IN LITERATURE: THE FINAL STAGE [1]

It seems possible to say that the course of literature obeys a principle of alternation and recurrence; that roughly similar frames of mind, with ever increasing variety of content, reappear at diminishing intervals; and that the rhythm of development in the older European nations, such as England and France, is even now approaching or reaching the stage of stability towards which the oscillations of the past inevitably tended. The spiral curve is coming to its completion, a final stop. Shall the metaphor prove valid to the very letter; and are we witnessing the advent of a period of stagnation, when the range of the driving power that kept the progress of thought active being more and more narrowed, the life of motion and change, and the zeal of fresh unadulterated impulses, must ebb away from literature?

It is a great while indeed since the world began to find itself ageing; and the surge of youth has daily given the lie to the prophecies of decay. But it does look as if the feeling of a protracted experience had sunk definitively into the consciousness of mankind.

[1] A lecture delivered in French at the Institut des Hautes Études, Brussels, in May 1927.

Some symptoms in the present phase of literary development would betoken that the sources of untapped vitality and actual renovation were beginning to fail. The interval is too short from one beat of the literary rhythm to another; it is increasingly difficult for the most complacent memory to forget that the enthusiasm and relief of to-day are but echoes of the similar enthusiasm which welcomed a different relief not long ago. There mingles a subtle sense of the *déja vu* with each new doctrine and watchword of art; and the eagerness of æsthetic reformers is secretly thrilled with the doubt that is born of a remembered ardor and disillusionment. When once the limit of sophistication was reached, there would be no margin left for the mere possibility of a change. All the moods and all the formulæ of literature would impregnate and interpenetrate one another. The seeds of every growth would lie indiscriminately together, entangling their roots as soon as they began to sprout. That consummation would be the more inevitable, for the convergence upon it of nature and the work of man: while on the one hand psychological heredity tended to enlarge the latent awareness of new generations, literary culture on the other, by instilling the knowledge of the past into young minds, would make it impossible for budding writers to think their own thoughts and speak their own words, without being conscious of the silent voices that had expressed those thoughts and uttered those words before.

It is easy to imagine the features by which the period of complete saturation would be known. Eclecticism would then be the prevailing habit of taste; and the course of literature would be at the same time uneventful and agitated, almost constantly broken by fitful actions and reactions, which vainly aimed at pushing somewhat further principles of art already stale and driven to extremes. Tendencies would be intermingled in confusion; contradictory characteristics in the same writers would be the rule; as the conscious and critical faculties exceeded the creative, the programs would bulk larger than the works; while the works themselves, owing to the predominant weight of vicarious mental experience, would most often thoroughly differ from the authors' actual endeavors.

Eclecticism, in fact, was the final stage through which the literatures of the past reached their extinction; and it is obvious enough that the signs of a mutual contamination of aims and tendencies are now rife, for example in the literatures of France and England, and to a lesser degree perhaps in other literatures. Stagnation, and a rapid jerky series of abortive attempts at a thorough change, are the apparently incompatible attributes of the present. The second romanticism of yesterday lingers out its life, still steeped to the core in the naturalism of a previous phase; while the effort toward a new classical ideal of form vainly tries to liberate itself from the persistent romanticism with which it is all instinct. The analysis of the inner world is made ever more realistic and accurate; but that exacting sense of truth hardly serves the cause of art, and the *surréalistes* have failed to do more than lead us to partial or complete unintelligibility. No genuinely fresh formula of the art of writing, even in the desperate attempts of this age, has thus far appeared; and small wonder, since it is difficult to fancy what it could be.

Are then the oldest literatures of Europe doomed to a swift decline and death? The inference is very wide, that would read such a decisive omen in the symptoms of the present day. To indulge in dismal prophecies seems particularly futile, when history teaches one thing clearly, that from past instances no safe conclusion can be drawn. The time was, when nations and literatures allowed themselves to die; what if the spiritual energy that animates them rose above that fate, and if the peoples transcended their destiny by taking it into their own hands? The literature of a given country cannot cease of itself; its substance not being its own, but that of a collective life, its course can be stopped only by the total breaking up of the mental activity that supported it. Now present-day cultures are gradually learning how to escape the threats of material or moral exhaustion; a social hygiene has been developed, and the span of national, like that of individual existence, has been much increased. While men must finally die, it is difficult to imagine how in normal circumstances a nation that wanted to remain intellectually active could be forced to see its vital flame quenched, if it had been wise enough to evade all destructive conflicts with the natural laws of health. The advance of psychology and of the social sciences is gathering up the body of knowledge that may renovate the energy of life through the practical art of living. It is not inconceivable that the will of peoples, thus guided, should save them from the ageing of their spiritual selves. And in many ways besides, the necessary power could happen to be developed, that would renew the vitality of the race, and make a fresh start possible. Socially for instance, through the better adjustment and cultivation of their individual units, or internationally, through the emergence of a peaceful order that would eliminate much waste, the modern nations might find themselves enough rejuvenated, to begin again the cycle of their mental development.

But above all, there is no decisive reason why we should be unduly obsessed by the findings of history and the data of the past. The rhythm of literature is no part of the divinely-appointed order of the universe. It has been; but that does not mean that it shall ever be. The alternate recurrence of major moods and artistic tones is an aspect of man's slavery to the infirmity of his own nature; it springs from the conditions of organic life, and its roots are in the body. It is not impossible to conceive that the weakening and final disappearance of the rhythmic succession of periods in literature might be the instrument, as it is a sign, of the further liberation of our spirit; a stage in the onward march of mankind.

It does not appear at all necessary that art should be controlled by fashion. The day might dawn when even enfranchised woman will reject her self-inflicted tyranny, and freedom in clothes will be claimed and won; when each person dresses according to his or her own sense of fitness. One wonders whether in literature, at least, we might not be standing upon the threshold of some such new world.

Eclecticism of taste in the past coincided with the final inertia of letters. But one has still to demonstrate that the two terms are inevitably associated. No necessity in reason or in fact demands that they should be so. On the contrary, it might be soundly argued that if the era of eclecticism is the last stage in the development of literature, that phase, contrary to previous experience, could henceforward be of indefinite duration and unchecked fertility.

It did in the past correspond with an exhausted vitality of the national mind. But what if the vitality were not exhausted? In itself, a broad tolerant sympathy of artistic taste is no unfavorable condition to creative work of a robust as well as widely varied quality.

What made it unlikely that an eclectic age should be very fertile, was the relative mediocrity of the average reader's psychological preparation for art; so that the cultivated man or woman's normal receptivity had to be strained, as soon as more than one type of æsthetic expression was to be accepted and enjoyed at the same time. But the reach and scope of ordinary minds is being gradually extended, although there may be no actual increase in the vigor of the greatest; and the reward of the present-day deepening and expansion of culture, the fruit of a prolonged psychological experience, seems to be a much more supple adaptation of the general public to various forms of art. That is of course the very state of things implied in the notion of eclecticism. But while the word usually called up the idea of a fastidiously indolent tolerance, the novel factor of the present is that the sensibilities of the young do not seem to be jaded, though they are perceptibly more elastic and open.

The condition that would have to be fulfilled in order to ensure, under those circumstances, the indefinite duration of a productive vitality in art and letters, is that the individual writer or reader were reinstated in the full enjoyment of his rights. The pressure that established schools and fashions and tones and modes of expression even now exercise on the creation and appreciation of books, would have to give way definitely to the principle of independence. At all epochs in the past of literature, it already was a fact that the greatest artists rose superior to the prevailing manner of their time; they were more or less synthetic and universal. But the privilege of the few should become, through the diffusion of a comprehensive culture, the birthright of the many. That freedom would be the more indispensable, as the subconscious mind of the new generation was more thoroughly saturated with the influence of bygone ages. Such an inheritance is a burden, and in a way tends to put a limit on our unrestricted motion; the corrective must be sought in the compensatory breadth of taste, in the many and varied possibilities that offer, both to the writer and the reader, so long as they do not lack the energy to move. Now to all appearances that liberation is taking place; its herald can be discovered in the fluctuating and incoherent attempts through which the old-time unity of style vainly tries, at the present day, to reassert itself.

The age of schools is past and gone; that of the individual creator or critic as the measure and basis of art has come in. The romantics claimed some such freedom; but their sense of a collective trend in æsthetic matters was stronger than their ideal of liberty, and they put a ban, in fact, on the classical preferences of taste. Exhausted in the field of abstract general moods, the principle of originality and renovation is finding a new domain in the unlimited range of subjective shades and of the concrete personal temperament. New combinations, in indefinite number, and of a practically boundless variety, can be effected between elements—themes, tones, attitudes, responses, techniques—none of which is in itself exactly untried and unfelt. Instead of being swayed by broad movements that ruled man's preferences from the outside, through the magnetism of some predominant appeal, and imperiously attuned all tastes to one major key, it is conceivable that the individual should claim his freedom, and obtain it by the very act of exercising it. Affinities thus would play over the whole extent of national—in an increasing number of cases, of international literature—and each sensibility would seek for sympathy by self-expression in complete tones, the vibrations of which would awake widely scattered echoes.

The very idea of schools and official doctrines of art thus being once for all renounced, much more store would be set than now by the unchecked development of personal instinct in the young—a principle of intellectual and æsthetic pedagogy which has been in fact winning gradual acceptance, and the recognition of which is even now deeply transforming education. The revolt of original artists and thinkers, at all times, against the authority of the reigning standard of taste, and the hostility of healthy minds to orthodox repositories of literature, would thus be justified. There never was a time when the greater writers were not more or less at odds with the traditional training which they had received; genius is self-made, just as surely as talent is at least partly made. Now the full connotation of the word genius has still to be realized; its meaning is personality.

Should the cry of anarchy be raised here? The preoccupation with standards has had its chance since the world began; and it seems clear at last that they have done more harm than good. It is the weakness of the human mind to hold by them as by the embodiment of economy of effort; and it is more useful now to relax than to strengthen their rule. That they serve a social end cannot be disputed; but their necessity as such is assuming a new character from the maturity and the prolonged experience of mankind. Every being is born to-day with the ingrained sense of the discipline which for thousands of years has been unceasingly enforced; the instinct of order and the craving for a common measure of intelligibility and beauty have become hereditary features. The full-grown spirit of man can now take the law unto itself, and play with the docile instrument which numberless generations have fashioned. The need of truth and spontaneousness and life is everything; life will call unto life, and new values be evolved from the natural analogy of tastes. The rule that sensibilities did not work out of themselves would be of no validity or service. The only genuine standards are those which correspond to the deep-laid insuperable conditions of our mental activity; those cannot be long ignored, and never are violated by artists with impunity; they should be left to assert themselves. The course of art is not to be

forcibly guided and bent in a direction prescribed
by an ideal of conformity or truth, once revealed
and ever supreme, unchanging and unchangeable.
In so far as such an ideal does exist, it is inscribed
in our very constitution, which alters and grows;
in so far as it does exist, it is making, and not made.
The times need a greater measure of the freedom
that is the privilege of art, not a stronger enforce-
ment of external rule.

For centuries the training of artists has centered
on the teaching of what was attempted and done
before. The lessons of the past are now in our
blood; how could our civilization be other than experienced and wise? What we lack is rather the
power of forgetting, and the illusion of believing
that the paths which we try are new. Let us at least
be ourselves; originality in the supreme sense is not
the gift of all, but sincerity can be. Whatever pedagogy may say as to the claim of the classical humanities, and whatever their efficiency may be in
shaping the minds of the young, they have long
ceased to be indispensable to the artist in words; the
essence of their example impregnates the achievements of the moderns. Futurism as a movement was
unnecessarily and noisily iconoclastic; but the cause
of futurism is to-day that of all sincere lovers of
art.

That the era of more unchecked freedom, thus
opening out before the writer, would be that of
cosmopolitanism and international culture, goes
without saying: it is only in the unlimited field of

supra-national civilization that the individual can possess his full responsibility and liberty; that he can display all the range of his appeal as man, and depend on no other means to make himself heard and accepted. It is plain enough that the problem of language stands upon the threshold of that prospect of a world literature, a formidable, a yet unremoved obstacle. How the words of a writer must remain national, while his thought, his feeling and his technique may be international, quite as much as they are personal, seems to point to the road along which a compromise is being tentatively sought. Neither our desires, nor our sense of the possible, can be reconciled at present to the utopian notion of a common language, cherished and used with intimacy of associations by all the families of man.

It is unhappily certain that being in some respects a privileged means of expression, fortunate in the range and wealth of its medium, literature is the most directly threatened of all arts by the growing sophistication and the ageing of our culture. That the periodicity which so long held sway over it is showing some signs of relaxing its hold, is not in itself an omen of evil. The inevitable eclecticism of contemporary taste does involve a risk; but the menace will prove ineffectual if the naïve thoughtlessness of youth refuses to see it or to take it seriously. Let the mature meanwhile lay their heads together, and try to realize the course of our spiritual destiny; beyond that they need hardly go: their most reasonable participation in the gradual unfolding of our æsthetic future does not much differ from a reflective and tolerant passiveness. Our young men and women will go on creating new art, if only their anxious elders are wise enough to let them be. The heat and burden of the day will then wear off; and mankind will awake one morning to find itself younger, because it had forgotten overnight that it was old.

PARALLELISM IN THE RECENT DEVELOPMENT OF ENGLISH AND FRENCH LITERATURE

PARALLELISM IN THE RECENT DEVELOPMENT OF ENGLISH AND FRENCH LITERATURE [1]

I

ANALOGIES AND RESEMBLANCES

I

There ever hides some other uninvited interest in our response to the appeal of a purely historical subject. Beyond the courageous expectation of enlightenment, our curiosity is stirred by that obstinate hope which attaches to the discussion of topics unrelated with our present purposes. Perhaps, we keep thinking, one of the real riddles, the consciousness of which is always with us, will be glanced at by luck; perhaps unexpectedly the deeper cravings of the mind will receive some slight nourishment. An emotional shade is thus added, at least potentially, to all inquiries; and the particular quality of that emotion, the nature of that secret background, is the most characteristic element in the temper of an age.

Ours is, and will remain, after the great upheaval, an era of shifting and readjustment. One of our

[1] The William John Alexander lectures, delivered at the University of Toronto, on January 28th, 29th and 30th, 1929.

permanent preoccupations to-day centers round the conflict between the claims of the nation and those of the race. This world of ours, which has grown of late so much smaller, is obsessed by two apparently incompatible desires; on the one hand, it labors still to endow with fuller reality those separate units of social and moral existence, the repressed nationalities, the provinces, the local groups, merged till now within a wider political aggregate; on the other hand, and more insistently yet, the clear or dim sense of unity is stirring at the heart of the various families of man. Whilst the modern nation, that product of the ages, to which the nineteenth century gave the finishing touch, is still, in many parts of the world, carried onward by its incompletely fulfilled aim, the outline of the new international order is sketching itself out from the chaos of the war. One tide being at the ebb, the other, which is rising, has to beat down its resistance; and the ensuing struggle, with its eddies and cross-currents, looks like the purposeless agitation of an angry sea. Such is the main cause of the complexities of the present years. A broad survey of the facts, and the vision of a hopeful mind, are needed to discern the superior surge which is gathering from the broken waters; to discover in national ardor itself the zeal that will sustain an all-embracing brotherhood.

No theme is more engrossing, no object is more worthy of our instinctive preference, than the prom-

ise of the reconciliation of mankind. In this new
world, where many nations live together like one,
there will be some indulgence for the audacity of a
student of literature, if he allows the glamor of
that dream to lure him away from the proper field
of his craft. It is in no other light that the parallel
developments of French and English letters during
the last fifty years will be here studied; through this
particular problem, which concerns only two of the
Western nations, that more general issue, the
growth of one European culture—the nascent soul
of the coming United States of Europe—may
perhaps not inappropriately be adumbrated.

II

It has been the task of comparative, or to speak
more properly of general literature, to establish the
broad fact of collective movements and cycles in the
intellectual history of Europe. Over the frontiers,
the barriers of speech, religion, blood and economic
interest, common promptings have made themselves
felt at all times. After the rise of modern nationalities had broken up the cosmopolitan culture of the
middle ages, the spirit of the Renaissance was
another unifying force, and its infection spread a
single mood from South to North, to West and to
East. After the political and religious conflicts to
which the Reformation gave rise, the eighteenth
century saw the radiating power of the philosophy
of enlightenment, and citizenship of the world was

in fashion. When the period of the French Revolution had ushered in a hundred years of fierce national rivalry, culminating in the last war, the present revulsion was let loose by the will to live of mankind.

Meanwhile, and all through those varying fortunes of the battle between the needs of the modern nation and the trend to some unity of culture, magnetic currents kept passing from one country to another; the spell of a school, an art, a personality, was again and again cast far and wide, shaping artists and writers in various lands to subtle analogies or resemblances. Out of the confused series of literary action and reactions, there emerge four main impulses, of successive and ever shorter duration: classicism, romanticism, realism, symbolism; and the full history of each would have to take in the whole of Europe, or indeed, with some notable exceptions, of the civilized world.

Those are the outstanding conclusions to be gathered from the merest survey of the past. Again, it is obvious at first sight that the literatures of France and England, if considered apart from the others in their parallel growth, show a special analogy of development. Not that those two nations, lying as they do close to each other and associated by so many bonds of situation, commerce and similar interests, are not parted by the widest differences of temper; so manifold and so deep is the opposition of their genius, that they have always found quite as good reasons for their frequent hostilities as for their sense of mutual esteem. Nature, and the political evolution of Europe, have laid on both sides of the English Channel seeds of estrangement even more prolific than those of love. But France was to England the gate of the Continent, and of the warm sensuous artistic South; England was to France the sea-girt home of a proud strange people, the gate unto the mist and the mysteries of the North; and they stood to each other in such a relation, that the spirit of classicism should always reach England through France, and that romanticism to France should be English before it was European. They were thus predestined, in spite of their glaring incompatibilities, to play predominant parts in each other's mental history.

That they did so is matter of common knowledge. The influences of French literature in England during the seventeenth, eighteenth, and nineteenth centuries, of English literature in France during the eighteenth and nineteenth, cannot be too much emphasized. They are not, of course, to be regarded as the sole cause of the analogies of development which obtained through that long period between one side of the Channel and the other. When England to all appearances followed France in adopting the classical standard of beauty founded on reason; when France apparently followed England in setting up the worship of romantic enthusiasm; when England, again, looked to France for

the pattern and the formula of an art that renounced enthusiasm and transferred its allegiance
to realistic truth, there could be no question of a
mere passive obedience to the powerful example of
a more precocious guide. Those changes, in so far
as they were deep and genuine, were rooted in the
spontaneous rhythm of national minds, secure
through the possession of themselves, even while
they lent themselves to the radiation of a foreign
genius. Still, the outlines of the two developments
evince a general analogy to each other; only they
are not, so to say, on the same plane. The accidents
of the curves are not exactly similar; and they do
not quite correspond in point of time.

The literary history of France and England, as
a whole, bears witness to the stubborn resistance
which the originality of the two nations offered to
the merging of their intellectual evolutions into one
process. Time differences are the more conspicuous,
for the general trend of the movements being more
obviously parallel. The classical age ripened in
France before it actually began in England; its
climax in England coincided with its decline in
France; the northern people was a pioneer on the
path to romanticism, the southern led the way to
realism. All through those centuries, the increasing
analogy between the cultures of the two nations
was not yet sufficiently marked to counterbalance
their diverging tendencies, and the unequal pace at
which they moved on their courses. The impression

of a difference is hardly less striking than that of a resemblance. The same phases, as they appear in both countries, borrow from their surroundings strong elements of discrepancy. The classical literature of England is not like that of France. French romanticism is comparable only in some respects to English; and the art of the French realists is not accurately reproduced even by such English writers as set out to imitate it. So broad, besides, is usually the time margin, that the whole tone and atmosphere of a school are necessarily altered, when after a while it has gained a safe footing on the land where it migrated. It could hardly be expected that the classicism of Pope would resemble in every essential that of Boileau or Racine; Europe, and the world, had kept moving on during the fifty odd years which parted the youth of one from that of the others; these belonged to the seventeenth, that to the eighteenth century.

The effect of those repeated accidents is to maintain between the two literatures a lack of symmetry that qualifies their parallelism. Besides, the relative scarcity of communication, and the small size of the reading public, allow an inventory to be made of the contacts which took place between the two nations; in most cases, the channels through which influence was brought to bear can be found and traced; the anteriority of one country to the other is beyond doubt; the initiatives taken, the appeals made, the responses given, and the personalities of the men or the individualities of the works through which every magnetism made itself felt, are recognizable; indeed they constitute the very materials with which comparative literature deals. The facts thus seem to bear out the assumption of a series of impulses originating in one center, and being thence transmitted to the other, even if the other had been independently preparing to receive it. In consequence, the idea of the definite action exerted by one country upon the other, remains in a central and privileged position; it throws into the shade the fainter recognition of a principle of similarity, ingrained in the mental progress of the two peoples, and working out to a more and more sure approximation of their spiritual fates. Those goddesses of orthodox literary history, influences, can thus be said to keep their ascendancy over the notion of a spontaneous affinity of cultures.

III

The aspect of the problem is gradually altered, as we pass on to the contemporary period—an age whose limits might be roughly marked out as from 1875 to our day. The symmetry between the two literatures is then emphasized; the analogies and resemblances to one country show themselves in the other almost at once, or after a brief interval; so intricate is the relationship, so many and so complex are the points where affinities appear and actions might be surmised, that the whole subject must be thenceforward viewed in a new light.

From 1875—a date chosen as a symbol, to denote a transition which spread over more than a decade—the intellectual condition of France and that of England have been growing more substantially similar. The traditional differences and oppositions are still felt, but they are no longer paramount; the discrepant elements seem to be rather attenuated, whilst those of harmony show a relative increase; the two countries, so to say, are falling into line with each other.

There was no suddenness about the change. The middle part of the century, in England as in France, had been an age of consolidation, when the vigor of romanticism, being half spent, had subsided, and yielded to a desire for a reconstructed moral world. Reason, as in the days of classicism, was again the watchword; but it was no longer the bold, confident logic of the uninformed mind; the material world was very much with man, and man's achievement centered in the knowledge and mastery of the world. Science was the power, long rising, now supreme, whose discipline guided the intelligence, and even controlled the imagination and the heart. In such an atmosphere, art would set before itself the very aim of scientific studies; and the time-honored doctrine of the imitation of nature, instinct with a new zeal and a spirit of stiff uncompromisingness, was again put forth under the name of realism. And yet, the romantic fire was not extinguished; it glowed still in the deeper recesses of the soul, irradiating the very fanaticism and the somber ardor of the apostles of truth. The literature and the thought of the age are thus rife with diverging attempts, which can best be organized under the common aim of a search for balance. French poetry with the Parnassians and the Victor Hugo of the "Légende des Siècles" obeyed promptings not dissimilar to those which actuated the careful artistry of Tennyson, and the psychological disquisitions of Browning. French fiction with Flaubert and Zola stood at an intellectual position, a more sober equivalent for which could be found in Thackeray and George Eliot. Matthew Arnold tried to be for England Sainte-Beuve and Renan in one.

Incomplete as it was, that relative analogy of content had itself been reached only by a gradual approach. From the beginning of the century, the lines of the two literatures were obviously tending to a closer parallelism. France indeed had reached the climax of the romantic age later than England; and the star of romanticism began to set with her at a later date. But the realism of 1850, which answered her genius more spontaneously, took hold upon her more strongly; and she thus overtook her neighbor on the way to the new ideal of truth. Pushing further and taking the lead, she evolved the formula of naturalism from a more drastic application of the principle of science to literature. At this extreme stage, the worship of frankness in art would meet of course with formidable obstacles in

the reticence and respectability of Victorian England; naturalism had to wait for a generation before
it could show itself without a mask on English
ground, although its action is perceptible even from
1880 in the more pungent and bitter flavor of some
significant works.

About 1875, the relation of France, and that
of England, to the two opposite principles of intellectual objectivity, and of free emotional expression, were largely the same. With both, the ra-
tionalist impulse had not spent itself; it was still
carried onward by its own impetus, and the prestige
of science remained intact. France had the positivist
school, and the followers of Comte; England had
the evolutionist philosophy of Spencer; with one
as with the other, there was no escape from the final
sway of a glorified common sense over life. Then it
was that the instincts of men began to turn away
slowly and silently from the lesson of a cold courage,
which had only brought bitterness and despair in its
train. A new age of the heart and the imagination,
a new intuitive age, was dawning; and in the reborn
hope and freedom of the soul, the lingering romanticism which dated back from the early century
linked up with the renascent romanticism of its close.

That liberation of the spirit was the outstanding
fact of the new period in the development of
thought and letters; it gave its most distinctive feature to the transition from the nineteenth to the
twentieth century. In France, where intellectual

movements are always more self-conscious, the reaction against science came more early to a head. Before 1880, Boutroux had struck the keynote of the new philosophy in divesting the so-called natural laws of the august absolute value with which man had fondly endowed them. Shortly afterwards, Bergson began to put forth his living active doctrine, one of the freshest, most stimulating suggestions ever offered to the mind of an age; and the scholar first, then the general reader, grew aware of a subtle change in the fabric of their inward experience. Objects were no longer hard and fast; the outlines of nature and the mental world ceased to be rigid; things flowed and melted into one another, and in the stream of consciousness all the facts of the inner life coalesced as smoothly and intricately as the particles of a liquid mass. When Brunetière drew the conclusion that had been forcing itself on many thinkers, voiced the disappointment of hopes which responsible scientists had never encouraged, and spoke of the bankruptcy of science, the thought of the time was ready for the catching phrase; it responded loudly; and the new century was born among the stirrings and searchings of a disquietude which tended either to traditional faiths, or to the breaking down of a hard belief, as depressing as unbelief and no less fixed than dogma.

The literature founded on science, meanwhile, was clinging to its tenets, apparently not without fair success; had it not gathered more and more documentary evidence, and was not the animality of man convincingly established? Through its burrowings into the obscure regions of the soul, however, and through the alliance which it struck with the radical criticism of society and life by foreign and chiefly Scandinavian writers, naturalism in some of its side-currents was undergoing a process of change; the fierce desire for truth was no longer contented with the findings of medical observation and social experiments; psychology was coming to the front as the chief revealer of the unknown in man; and the spirit of objective subservience to facts found itself strangely permeated with a kind of mysticism. Maupassant was obsessed by the thrill of the supernatural; the disciples of Ibsen and the men of the "Théâtre Libre" associated the crudest realism with flights of imaginative poetry. Springing from many sources at once, a new romanticism was welling up; in it the most diverse elements loosely mingled; the revolt against science and a too positive world, a reassertion of the rights of fancy, mystic beliefs, a craving for the unexperienced and the new, associated with the stern spirit of naturalism into a lawless search for intensity. Villiers de l'Isle Adam and Barbey d'Aurevilly had bridged over the gap from the old romanticism to the new; but already their romantic defiance was flavored with a spice of decadentism; and the end of the nineteenth, the early years of the twentieth century saw a medley of artists and writers, at one in nothing but in a desperate search for novelty, celebrating indiscriminately the cult of the most sordid truth, and that of the most spiritual illusion; naturalists, or æsthetes, or symbolists, and all more or less decadents.

To the complexities of that literary age, Symbolism holds the master key. From a quickened sense of the autonomy of mind, and of the fresh wonders which consciousness held in store, a new poetry had sprung, as free and original as if science had not tried to make the world regular, monotonous and dull. Imagination was the queen of an art which aimed at seizing and suggesting elusive intuitions. Over and above their power of direct normal statement, words were found to possess a mysterious value, born of their associations, of the images they called up, and chiefly of their sound. Language obeying subtle laws of rhythm became the instrument of a music which conveyed a spell potent enough to satisfy all the needs of intelligence. Whilst the grand symphony of Wagner, the poignant chords of Debussy, were keeping up through the age a fever of musical enthusiasm; whilst the impressionist painters decomposed color into flashes of light, and individual objects into vibrations of color, the school of Baudelaire, Mallarmé, Rimbaud, Verlaine turned poetry into a witchcraft. Its appeal was now wholly to the beyond, and it expressed nothing but the inexpressible; it was rich with the difficult visions of the seer, the wild outpouring of the ecstatic heart, or the tender effusive simplicities of the child.

French literature on the eve of the war was, as it has remained since, in a state of confusion, or perhaps one could more properly say a state of fusion. The various tendencies which had successively, through a long history, taken the lead and lost it were still present and obscurely at work in the mind of an age more complex than any other; all the doctrines of art were represented in the tentative efforts of groups too numerous or too ephemeral to rally around them the purposes of the time in a permanent way. If a formula must be singled out, in order to grant the period a character of its own, no doubt the writers who claimed as their standard the rejuvenated principle of classicism, should be selected. But the new classicism of the École Romane, of Maurras, Gide, Valéry, has hardly more than a general trend in common with that of the seventeenth century. It is divided from the faith of an unsophisticated age by the accumulated experience of three centuries. France seems to have entered the phase of literary eclecticism, when all doctrines are accepted, and no binding rule is in force; when the individual writer has won for himself an unlimited scope, and productive temperaments are to be found scattered all over the range of possible expression.

The condition of English literature during the same period could be sketched out in terms not indeed identical, but fairly similar. Soon after 1875,

England saw a revolt of thought and art against all the disciplines, mental or moral, which had threatened the independent life of the spirit; and the twentieth century began in a strong reaction aimed frankly at the authority of the nineteenth. Dogmatic science, a narrow intellectualism, a materialist smugness, a canting respectability, were denounced as various aspects of one central evil, the Victorian tradition. Idealism was reasserted in philosophy; and the pragmatists, who were nothing if not realists, claimed to be champions of spiritual values because they laid stress on the vital utility of faiths. Samuel Butler, the author of "Erewhon", brought to bear such a sharp irony on social and religious conventions, that his satire took destructive effect on the religion itself of science; his evolutionism was not Darwinian, but Lamarckian; he reinstated intuition as a privileged approach to knowledge, and seized in man's vital impulse that essential memory which is mind. A keen critic of his time, Meredith was no less a leader of the idealist revolt; his highest message was a lesson of free supple intuitive thinking. Meanwhile the Victorian order was even more directly assailed by the pessimists in its self-satisfaction, the source of its inmost strength; and Hardy began to build up his novels like massive austere entrenchments, from which his sad glance surveyed nature and the world of man.

That genuine life of English letters, the romantic inspiration, which had entered as a leaven into the very dignity of Victorian art, was stimulated afresh in the rebellion of the declining century; and through the manifold expressions of the new romantic eagerness, the spirit of symbolism breathed everywhere like a diffused essence. Dante Gabriel Rossetti was already a symbolist poet in everything but the name; Swinburne was another: the flood of his verse poured forth in a rush of rhythm and sound, guided by a haunting cadence, and urged on by the ardor and the bitterness of the senses. Robert Louis Stevenson, disgusted with the realism of Zola, instilled the soul of romance into stories of reality and tales of adventure. Nevertheless, the naturalist impulse, which was in spite of all gaining acceptance, combined itself with other and at times strangely alien desires and revolts; the "yellow nineties" saw the æsthetes, the decadents, and the Celtic revivalists, express in various guise the dissatisfaction of their hearts, yearning for intensity and beauty, for the sensational and crude, the rare and abnormal, or the dreams of a mystic imagination. The age of Oscar Wilde and John Davidson was as well that of Francis Thompson and W. B. Yeats.

The obstinately ethical genius of England would not dwell for long in the wilderness of decadence; and the reaction of the rallying purposes set a firmer stamp of doctrine on the opening decades of the twentieth century. As French literature possessed the school of Barrès and the traditionalists, side by side with the ironical criticism and the hu-

manitarian faith of Anatole France, English letters
had the imperialists and the believers, the school of
Kipling and that of Chesterton, along with the logical passion that feeds the satirical drama of Shaw.
The tender impressionism of Galsworthy is pregnant with a philosophy of charity, whilst the robust
realism of H. G. Wells works up to an illumined
human hope.

The present years are proverbially difficult to ex-
plore; the wood cannot be seen for the trees. In the
swarming life of English letters to-day, are any
symptoms visible, as in France, of a return to some
formula of balance, composure and classicism? Such
signs indeed abound, and could be pointed out in the
cool detached irony of a Strachey, the dry elegant
manner of an Aldous Huxley, in the fashionable interest which again attaches to the style and the life
of the Augustan ages of Dryden and Pope. But the
fever of an anxious thought still burns under the
affected cynicism or indifference; and through the
shifting play of tones and temperaments our predominant impression remains one of endless variety.
No clearly marked unifying principle is apparent;
England, like France, has entered the era of literary
individualism, and of composite, eclectic tendencies.

Such are the facts, in so far as they can be surveyed at so short a glance. That sketch, tentative as
it is, inevitably raises a further question: What of
that parallelism seemingly growing between the
literatures of France and England? How far is it to

be accounted for, and what may be its significance? Should it be explained by reciprocal influences? Can it be traced to a common background of civilization and culture? Or must we fall back upon another and a more spontaneous process, the nature of which we are not yet able clearly to define?

II

MUTUAL INFLUENCES AND THE COMMON BACKGROUND

If, as seems to be the case, there exists a marked analogy of general trend between the recent literatures of England and France, one is tempted to account for it by laying stress on the mutual influences that link up the two countries. It may appear obvious that the points of greater resemblance, with each, are those where the action of the other is taking effect; and that those points are now more numerous and more essential, simply because there are more French writers and thinkers appreciated in England, and English in France.

That is certainly part of the truth. Resemblance, if not caused, can be helped and encouraged from the outside. And the fact is that history shows us but few countries united by a closer relationship than that which has been prevailing between France and England, in the intellectual domain, for about half a century. Contact, indeed, is now fully established. A wide public on each side is kept in touch with the development of the other literature. All important books published in one country are brought in the other to the notice of a circle which may be small, if the interest of the work is technical, but is at times as large as, or larger than, the audience at home. Failing a translation, the foreign book can be read by many in its own words—a fair knowledge of one modern language having become a pretty common thing, and French in England, English in France, enjoying a privileged position. The point need hardly be labored; it is, in fact, a question of degree only, an almost equal intimacy of intercourse obtaining between most of the Western nations, especially when in direct proximity to each other.

The influences of individual writers, or of movements and groups, are in that general exchange like centers of greatest activity, whence the foreign genius radiates out over the public at large. The laws governing the selection of the writers and works that act most efficiently are complex enough, and can no more be laid down with accuracy, than the rules of success in any market; whether at home or abroad, the wind of literary favor cannot be safely forecast, and will blow where it listeth. But observation shows that imported books succeed mostly for one of two reasons—either because they find a ready response, and strike chords which easily vibrate; in other words, because they are not very different from the home produce; or for the very opposite motive, because being new and strange, they answer a curiosity and a dimly felt need of the mind. The former case is one of positive, the latter of negative and complementary affinity; but affinity is the key to both, and this fact throws a flood of light on the inner nature of the whole process.

From 1875 to the war, the tale of reciprocal influence between France and England is a long one. There is hardly an important movement or group of writers, on one side, that has not been more or less influential on the other; the quantity and quality of that action, its quicker or more delayed rise, and its duration, depending on individual factors, and offering an extremely wide range of variety. In this as in every field of the same kind, several planes, so to say, are to be distinguished, of increasing depth, and almost always of decreasing surface; the most popular foreign books being commonly of rather shallow interest, and appealing to the least cultivated class of readers. The extension of an influence, and its artistic fecundity, are thus often in inverse proportion to each other. The reception given in England to each French author of note, and conversely, is a particular problem, to be worked out independently. The map of those currents and cross-currents cannot of course be drawn until comparative literature has covered the period with a dense network of special studies.

A few illustrations, however, might be given; and first, as to French influence in England. Leaving out the most widely read books, and the fortune of second rate fiction for instance—a chapter of literary history well worth writing, for the sake of its contribution to the story of the passing of the Victorian order—it is possible to say that the more important French movements have all told, more or less rapidly and lastingly, on the English artistic conscience, and the élite of readers and writers. The naturalists had their followers in England, and the effect was no less deep for being restricted and retarded. From George Moore to Somerset Maugham, the example of Zola and Maupassant left its mark on English literature, and Kipling himself owed something to the French master of the short story. The symbolists were received on the whole more willingly, in spite of their often shady personalities; Baudelaire, the master of them all, awoke a long and profound resonance among the poets, and Swinburne was his enthusiastic disciple. The decadents of the "yellow nineties" were full of the spirit of Verlaine and Huysmans. Who would think of certain chapters of Wilde's "Dorian Gray" apart from "A Rebours"? Writers who harked back more plainly to the romantic tradition were no less successful. Daudet, whom his compatriots would call a French Dickens, was cherished by the British for his sentiment, and for his humor. Loti's romanticism of exotic moods stirred a response in other sensibilities than that of Lafcadio Hearn. When the new idealism was in the air, France had the privilege to give it its most striking expression, and Bergson left a deep imprint on the philosophy of England. The *école romane,* the

group of the traditionalists and that of the neo-
classicists have mattered less to the British as bodies
of doctrinaires than as sets of individual talents;
but many among them have a hold upon the élite,
and rank with the deep-felt literary forces of the
present. Barrès had his admirers, Proust has his
enthusiasts, and Valéry has received perhaps his fin-
est tribute of praise from an English pen; whilst
that intellectual symbolist, Mallarmé, whose cloudy
genius remains so near to us, has now at last come
into his own in England. Of the younger men, with
the newer programmes, it would be hard to name
one, whose personality had proved of more than
transient interest, who was not eagerly watched and
studied in the parallel circles of English writers.

It is hardly needful to add that French influence,
during that period, was most often of a general
kind; many minds in England, and not among the
less eminent, stood in discipleship not to such or
such a school or doctrine, but to some peculiar
quality of the French genius. Meredith loved the
Gallic clearness and bravery of wit; Stevenson, who
objected to Zola, took in many lessons from gentler
models of the French art of style; and who will
measure the indebtedness of Joseph Conrad to the
language and literature he knew so well? Who will
gauge the subtle effect of French intellectual courage, and of that definiteness of outline which is part
and parcel even of French impressionism, on the
manner of Galsworthy in "The Island Pharisees" or

"The Patrician"? It must not be forgotten, either, that the influence of a national mind is a massive force, deriving much of its impact from its tradition in time, and not exclusively from its contemporary exponents. The whole body of a foreign literature, present and past, is active at any moment upon such temperaments as may be fitted to respond to it; and for instance the cumulative effect of French analysis and style, from the seventeenth and eighteenth century masters down to Anatole France, is to be felt in the preference of taste which led some recent English essayists and novelists—such as Lytton Strachey, Aldous Huxley—to a decided reaction in favor of a neo-classic attitude. Now, the present, in that bent of taste, enters for as much as the past; it is partly through Anatole France that Racine and Marivaux have been reached.

The list, summary as it is, and limited to the barest mention of outstanding centers of influence, is imposing enough. But what is one to infer from it? Not, certainly, that the course itself of English literature was perceptibly modified by the magnetism of the French example. As soon as one leaves the domain of form, of manner and the technique of art, to probe to the deeper sources of inspiration, it is found that the thought of an age, its very temper, are implied in the choice it makes of such or such literary expressions. Now that temper is and must be primarily of independent, spontaneous growth. The lessons which French influence taught

England cannot be held responsible for those broader and more profound determinations of the spirit which make up the main changes of taste and feeling.

In fact, a somewhat closer sifting of the dates will qualify our previous impression. Did the French really implant naturalism on English soil? England had long had the mood of realism in her mental constitution; and that mood would be stimulated by the pressure of the scientific enthusiasm of the sixties and seventies. But the barrier which opinion and manners raised against complete frankness of treatment prevented the full acceptance of the uncompromising ideal of truth. "Jude the Obscure", in 1896, was still banned by the censorship of the readers. Even then, however, the dam had begun to give way, and the stream by degrees made its way through. If in the twentieth century reticence has become almost a thing of the past, is it because in the eighties and nineties translations of Zola sold so well, in spite of the press, the critics and the courts of law? A new generation had been assailing the Victorian order, and on all hands the strict discipline of former days was being upset. In this broad change, all the modern history of England, and all her contemporary life were concerned. To account for the vein of naturalism in recent English letters, one should stress native forces first: all those subtle transformations of mind, intimately bound up with social and intellectual experience, which weakened the hold of Puritanism, and opened the way for candor in the statement of unpleasant truths. One should not forget, either, the action of other literary influences than that of the French naturalists. French fiction, in that whole process, thus played an important, but still a secondary part. Other probings of the facts would yield similar results. The reversion of English thought to philosophical idealism began before the great French spiritualist, Bergson, could be known and appreciated in England. The tendency to symbolism showed itself in English poetry sooner than it did in French. The reaction against the decadence of the nineties appeared in England earlier than in France. . . .

The caution is the better founded, as the converse influence of English thought and literature upon France was proving, at the same time, no less active; and indeed, it brought to France, often enough, the very seeds France had sown; on occasion, before France could have sown them. . . . The network of comings and goings, of giving and receiving, at times, is so close and dense, that anteriority would be very hard to assign; the blessed word influence simply denotes the fact that modes of thought and feeling were somehow in the air of Europe.

An outstanding aspect of the period 1875-1914 in France is that the French genius then really discovered the original claims of modern English poets. Byron, Thomas Moore and Scott had had their day among their French contemporaries; Wordsworth had appealed to Sainte-Beuve; but it was only the symbolists of 1880 who felt the spell of Shelley and Keats. One of the main changes that have taken place in French poetry during the last fifty years is its approximation to an ideal of freely flowing sound and of intimate poignancy, the very reverse of rhetoric; and in the exploration of that new realm, the domain of musical suggestion, the symbolists were guided by the example of the English; one might say, of the Anglo-Saxons, as America took a share in the initiation: the haunting melodies of Poe, the grand marching songs of Whitman, played a part second to none in the awakening of the French ear to the power of weird, wistful or rousing verbal music, sustained by adequate rhythm. Verlaine was in actual contact with English poetry; Mallarmé's mind was deeply tinged with his English studies; and men whose native language was English, like Viélé-Griffin and Stuart Merrill, figured among the French symbolists.

In that closely interwoven pattern, reciprocal influences sometimes converge on one and the same spot; before Bergson was known and reverenced in England, he was himself profoundly a disciple of English philosophy; that some of his views, unknown to him, have been anticipated by Samuel Butler, is no mere accident. Speaking generally, the new romanticism of the English eighties and nineties fell in, as it was gradually known, with the mood of a period in French literature largely attuned to the same major key. When Meredith, after 1900, was discovered by a distinguished circle, what they appreciated was not so much his keen analysis as the imaginative flashing of his mind—the complementary, the English aspect of his genius. The sense of romance, the stress laid on adventure, the originality of themes, background and imagery, won a public much more easily and rapidly for Stevenson. The element of realism in Kipling was not the motive of his very wide popularity with French children and grown-ups alike; it was the thrill of his stories packed with energy, wonder and the mystery of strange worlds. Hardy gained a slower recognition through the somber intensity of his tragic imagination, not through his kinship with some features of the naturalist school. The recent success of Conrad is due to similar causes.

English influences in France would be ever on the romantic side; only, the romanticism may be cheap and shallow, or it may be the reverse. English novels in the French mid-nineteenth century enjoyed a moral and sentimental character; they belonged to the family circle, and the daughters of the respectable middle-class had their personal libraries stocked with them. On a superior plane, the action of English literature since that time, through the age of cosmopolitan reading which France has entered, has mostly been in favor of that imaginative idealism which is, under various forms, the predominant trait of the period. Even the realism of English novelists, from George Eliot to Arnold Bennett, brought to French readers other lessons than that of mere subservience to fact, and well could Brunetière set up the spirit of Eliot's art in a contrast with the naturalist school. Down to the present day, the note of warm zeal and prophecy in English letters has kept its hold on the French public. The critics of society, and the apostles of a better world, Shaw, Wells, Galsworthy, Chesterton, have awakened such a response among the reflective youth of France, that they may have left a mark on the thought of many.

Of late, however, the situation has somewhat changed; the freer inspiration of English writers since the nineties has called up an affinity with some of the more sophisticated French talents. Wilde, nurtured on French symbolists and decadents, was eagerly read by the French æsthetes. Among professed admirers of English literature, acknowledging its influence in a general way, one could mention, not only an Angellier or a Paul Bourget, but a Marcel Schwob, a Proust, an André Gide, a Valéry-Larbaud. Nearer to us, some of the boldest attempts at a new technique of writing have been elaborated in circles where Paris, London and Dublin meet on a footing of indiscriminate equality. Mr. Joyce would be teaching the French to what length the principle of discontinuity can be pushed, if the "surréalistes" had not found it all out before. . . . In him, the latest-born wonder and climax of modernism, the intricacy and immediacy of literary exchanges at present are well illustrated; what he owes to France is almost indistinguishable from what France owes to him. And what shall we say to the rise of Mr. Y. Green, that distinguished novelist whom French has won over from English, as Conrad was won over by English from Polish or French?

Let those names stand as indexes to many more. They may be sufficient to establish the fact of a closer interrelation than ever between the literatures of the two countries. But again the question arises: why and how were those influences possible? They are themselves an effect as much as a cause. No genuine influence takes place unless there is a preëxisting affinity; whether the personality that receives likes what is offered because already known and appreciated, or, more often, obeys a desire for what it has not, and a sense of need. The mind only assimilates what is fit to be its nourishment; and our sensibilities react only to such calls as awake their dormant powers. The problem thus recedes further back: what is there in the material and moral circumstances of our time, that can explain the growth of a reciprocal readiness to react, of a virtual sympathy and kinship, in the collective consciousness of both England and France?

That some part of the explanation should be looked for in the changed circumstances of the time, goes without saying. Present-day civilization has multiplied contacts among the different national groups, beyond the dream of yesterday. It is not immaterial to our purpose that communications from one country to the other should have become so easy and rapid; that books, magazines, newspapers should so quickly and naturally make their way over the English Channel; that through the telegraph, the telephone, the wireless, a simultaneity of mental and nervous reaction to the life of the whole world should have been established—France and England partaking of the same emotions over international events, and the more important of their home issues, as they arise; that men and women should come and go in such numbers between the two countries; and that so many on each side should have fresh personal impressions of things and people on the other. Through the actual presence of residents, travelers and tourists, substantial parts of England and of France enter into daily intercourse—the meeting since the war taking place usually on French soil. This is only a chapter in the great modern book of the canceling of distance through means of transport—a theme too general, and commonplace, to require much comment here. But perhaps it is to the point to add, that among the objections made on the English side against the proposed Channel tunnel, some refer, not absurdly, to the mental and moral as well as to the military aspects of the matter. . . .

But this, once more, cannot be the final answer to our query. That travelers, books and ideas are conveyed easily, safely and quickly from one to the other country, would not much signify, unless there was a desire on both sides to exchange them; unless there was a solidarity of mental interests; and this is bound up, naturally, with the solidarity of other interests as well. Here it is that we must take into account the whole subject of the present-day intercourse of nations. The relationship of England and France is part and parcel of the new nexus between human groups; and how closely woven that nexus is, it would be unpardonable to forget. From trade in material goods to the spread of theories and beliefs, most activities contribute to the strengthening of the links that bind up European peoples into a complex unit. The process, indeed, cannot be examined locally; it does not obtain more especially in the interrelation of England and France; it is a European, to a large extent a world fact. The interdependence of nations on the economic plane, the rise of international production, exchange and finance, an outstanding element of the present situation, need not be emphasized. The faint lineaments of a political organization have appeared at the same time; there is a League at Geneva, the British Empire has become a "Commonwealth of Nations"; and the "United States of Europe" is no longer quite so startling a phrase as it was fifteen years ago. The indirect bearing of our modest inquiry on that great issue is, avowedly, one of the motives that prompted it. But conversely, it must be pointed out that the growth of a practical solidarity among peoples might be the general cause, from which the closer parallelism of French and English literary developments would spring as a consequence.

There is weight, of course, in the argument; still, it is not conclusive. By the side of the connection thus emphasized, there is room for other factors. The gradual rise of the new European order is not a determining force, acting irresistibly, and from the outside, upon the spiritual progress of nations. To all appearances, on the contrary, this progress is a distinct growth, intimately associated with that movement, but not commanded and controlled by it.

No doubt, the number and the power of the collective rhythms that sway the lives of nations, are on the increase; the complete individuality and isolation which characterized the sovereign state of yesterday, gradually vanish before our very eyes. It is no wonder that in an age of world leagues, international organizations and business combines, the tides of artistic or literary fashion should succeed one another more quickly, and reach further away. Civilization is being unified; the ways of living, working, eating, dressing, traveling, change from the endless variety of local and national habits to a kind of cosmopolitan sameness. What more natural than that one mode of thinking and feeling should spread across the frontiers; that waves of preference in intellectual things should run more and more freely over the world; and if the moods of literature in Paris and London do converge, is that any more than an eddy of the great current which brings Asia into line with Europe and America industrially, politically, socially; and of that general leveling up of national originalities, through which Japanese painters, for instance, are adopting Western technique?

Indeed, what takes place between England and France is no exception. But we must still ask ourselves, whether those countries do not illustrate that world movement in a signal manner; and whether no other forces can be found at work in the process, than those which have been so far examined.

It was acknowledged at the beginning of this enquiry that the neo-romanticism or symbolism (in a broader sense) which can best serve for a general characteristic of the period from 1875 to 1914 had the amplitude of a Continental movement. Whilst the development of literature in England and in France during that period offers remarkable analogies, the same might be said, to some extent, of other European nations. For instance, German writers from 1880 to the war lent themselves to a rough grouping under similar heads; the life of letters for those thirty-five years consists mainly in a reassertion of the individual imagination, dealing with symbols, against the objective ideal of the naturalists; moreover, the swing back from impressionism and expressionism, after the war, to a self-possessed sense of form, would fit in well with the neo-classic reaction that is now active in France and discernible in England. In the same way, the literature of Italy from 1870 to our day might be very summarily outlined as a transition from the classical rhetoric of Carducci and the naturalism of Verga to a neo-romantic medley of diverging tendencies, the most typical of which would be the intuitionist æsthetics of Croce, the "futurists", and the "twilight" school of poetry; after which the claims of classicism and form had to be reasserted by the "Ronda" group.

The existence of broad lines of evolution, common to the modern literatures of Europe, with national accidents and irregularities traceable to local influences, would thus be once more established. But this test no less clearly supports our initial impression, that the similarity between the courses of contemporary literature in France and England had itself no exact parallel. The analogy is not so clear or the correspondence so close in the case of Germany; the period there is altogether more confused; stronger elements of variety and difference persist in the robust originality of the provincial spirit, in the intellectual paradox of a nation which is at once old and young, young through its impatient and seething vitality, old through its sharing in the most advanced European thought. With Italy, the case is even more complex; the vitality being still more eager and self-conscious, the sense of antiquity and of classical origins, on the other hand, more emphatic, while the struggle, even more violent, between the national unity and stubborn provincial traditions results in a more irregular line of advance.

The relationship between England and France is thus seen to escape, partly at least, the relative determinism of a generalization on experience; an element of particularity, something unique, is reintroduced into it; and under cover of the flexibility and margin which that individuality permits, we pass on to the more properly psychological or spiritual data of the problem.

After all, the course which a nation's literature takes is the surest index to the progress of its thought and feeling; and this has the attributes of a personality which develops: its present can always be connected with its past, since each moment sums up the experiences that were lived before; but no determinism hides in that connection, since to account for the present of a person with certainty, a knowledge of all the moral events leading up to it were necessary. Collective as well as individual minds are thus autonomous, in being to that extent self-determined.

The psychological history of England and France is long and full. It has advanced according to a rhythm, which in itself is impersonal, belonging more or less to all national groups. The swing from a classical to a romantic mood, and back again, has

governed the evolution of French and English literature since the middle ages. The same alternation, in
more or less similar form, has given their central
impulse to other European literatures; and in the
relative synchronism of those oscillations, the
general unity of Europe as one intellectual organism
has its cause, its promise and to some extent already
its being. But the mental rhythm of a given nation
is ever original; the precise quality of the inner elements it starts from, the particular incidents that
cross its career, and every part of its accumulating
record, are colored with its unique personality; and
thus the more marked approximation of English
letters to a parallelism with French literature does
reveal, over and above a certain community of general conditions, residing in a similar civilization and
culture, an analogy of will and purpose, and indeed
what one must call a spiritual affinity. This opens
the way to further aspects of the subject, with the
study of which our survey will come to a close.

Meanwhile, we are driven back to the conclusion that when all is said, one is faced in the field
of international, as in that of national psychology,
by a process of independent growth, or of a growth
which one must regard as independent. There is no
escaping from the inference that neither the spiritual climate, made up of mutual influences in the
domain of mind, nor the social climate, made up of
common features and tendencies in economic and
political life, can entirely account for the slow grad-

al ripening of an analogy in the consciousness of ations, revealed through the similar lines of their sychological development. We have to deal here, t seems, with a polarization of collective personalities to one central focus, and, so to say, with the action of a superior magnetism, which we must notice ut cannot properly explain. If there is a purpose unning through history, here is probably one of the oints where we lay a finger upon it; we witness at he present day a coming together of mankind; nd whilst it takes place chiefly through the gradual pening of individual minds to the claims of the osmos, it shows itself as well in the inward change f those collective beings, the personalities of na- ions, which are not simply the sum of the units hat make them up.

III

THE TREND TOWARD A EUROPEAN CULTURE

I

Comparing the recent course of literature in Eng
land and in France, with that in Germany and Italy
we seemed to notice that the analogy between th
two former countries was rather more marked tha
between them and the latter; and the main reaso
for the difference, we thought, was obvious enough
France and England, as unified human groups, wit
a continuous mental life, had a longer past.

This matter of age is here of decisive import
England and France are old nations. The epithe
does not bear any pejorative sense; no hint is con
veyed by it of weakness or degeneracy. But ten cen
turies of increasingly complex activity have bee
added to their remembered experience. In thei
moral selves, a complete cycle of evolution has bee
registered. With both, the rhythm of psychologica
development, through the shortening of its beat
and the capitalization of its phases, has reached a
stage of synthetic equilibrium. Theirs is that perioc
of collective life when, every fresh range of literary
invention having been already tried, really new de
partures are hardly possible; when individual tem

178

perament is the measure of everything, and writers are free to be themselves, if only they please. That condition of relative repose is not one of stagnation; it is probably final, which does not mean that it puts an end to literature. The eclecticism of taste which allows all natural gifts to grow is compatible, on the contrary, with prolonged and unchecked fertility.

The fact that the two countries have reached this stage of spiritual experience practically together, does in itself create a bond of similarity between them. But the quality of the stage is no less essential, in this respect, than its mere existence. There is in the ageing of nations a mellowness, as with men. The reward of a long life well lived is a gentle spirit of intelligent and forgiving humanity. France and England seem to have reaped that harvest of hard-won wisdom. The eclectic phase of literary development puts a ban on no mood, no style, no technique of expression; and such breadth of the artistic conscience is the token of a deeper tolerance of the spirit. It is possible to discern in both countries the signs of that maturation of the soul, which fits a collective self for the amenities and the sacrifices of social life. In that disposition, there resides perhaps the promise and the hope of the temper that will make the comity of Europe and of the world a reality.

The close understanding which has been established between England and France is, as it were, the first fruits of that inner disposition. On both

sides, serious allowances had to be made. Those of
political nature were uppermost in the public eye;
but the "Entente Cordiale" would not have lasted
for twenty-five years, and would not still offer every
sign of durability, unless there had been at play a
deeper will of mutual concession between the peoples
themselves. That such a pact was silently made is one
of the great facts in the modern history of Europe.
If reciprocal esteem has sufficiently warmed into
friendship to resist the wear and tear of daily fric-
tion, it is not only owing to the common sufferings
of the war; there has been an act of will also, a
consent given. And of that consent, tolerance was
the indispensable means. The old barriers of pre-
judice and ignorance have been to some extent over-
come; a quicker sense of the other nation's personality has been roused in the collective consciousness
of each. It was not done in a day. Pioneers were at
work on each side; the distorted image which the
hostility of generations had drawn was smoothed
down and corrected; a rough comprehension replaced
mutual unfairness and spite. France and England
learned to misunderstand each other less because
they underwent a change in their own selves. The
France of the twentieth century, with a character
sobered and instructed by suffering, with a more
serious outlook, was not impervious to the moral
earnestness of her neighbor; the England of the post-
Victorian age, eager for a freer and franker life
of the spirit, could own to herself the attraction of

French candor, without feeling a secret sense of guilt. Genuine sympathy with a few, mere acceptance with most, now spring from the very perception of what used to be an incompatibility; knowledge and experience have prompted a realization, however vague, of the psychological gain to be reaped from a broader contact, an inkling of the truth that two national minds so strongly opposed in most respects are complementary to each other. In so far as each nation is aware of itself, and of the other, it dimly feels that difference, once bridged over, is the way to mutual enrichment.

The Entente Cordiale is thus the possible type of a new kind of international agreement, the full acceptance by a human group of the existence of another, with its good qualities and defects, for better or for worse—an association that rather resembles modern marriage . . . The Entente was willed by the governments; but the peoples have sanctioned it, and so made it indestructible. History shows us few previous examples of such a conscious victory of reason over instinct. It possesses a rich psychological significance, and a wealth of possibilities. Its inner principle has an elasticity, a power of being extended to new problems and further relationships of the same kind. It bids fair to become one of the main centers from which the spirit of genuine tolerance will radiate out over circles of broadening humanity. Other centers of paramount importance, one need hardly add, would be the political wisdom evolved by the British Commonwealth of Nations, in its internal growth; and the federal spirit so fruitfully exemplified by the United States of America. And should the attempted understanding between France and Germany prove to be, as it may in the long run, a sincere reconciliation of the two peoples, the hope of mankind would find there an encouragement of equal value.

Through the atmosphere of more genial intercourse which the Entente has fostered, the intellectual relationship of France and England has naturally become more intimate still; the closer interdependence and analogy of their literary developments owes something, no doubt, to that favorable influence, which was first political, and tends to become social and moral.

II

We may pause here, and wonder whether a problem of general literature, followed out through its implications, has not brought us dangerously near to the plane of mystic argument.

There is nothing mystical, however, about these reflections, in so far as they take stock of the facts, and only probe them, or prolong them a little way. That some of their aspects are to be perceived intuitively, is a risk, but one that may well be faced. The most solid realities, and the most vital, in the history of literature, cannot be perceived otherwise.

What are the facts? That if we take literary development to be a broad index to the inner life of nations, there has been in modern times, and more especially during the recent period, an approximation of the collective mind of England to that of France, and conversely. A certain parallelism in the main movements of letters has resulted, rather more marked than that which obtained with other Western literatures. This special feature can be accounted for by the circumstances of the time, but it cannot be explained away. No doubt, the same general conditions of civilization prevail in both countries; they have both been subjected to the same currents of European influence; their proximity makes them of particular significance in each other's mental growth; almost all the writers of note on one side have been more or less known and appreciated on the other. That interdependence has increased still with the facilities of communication, and the spread of cosmopolitan tastes. Lastly, the social history of the two countries shows that their national consciousness became adult about the same time, so that their moral experience went through similar phases, and they have reached together a stage of psychological maturity. Still, the succession of the beats in the English and French rhythms, even during the nineteenth century, was not identical; and at the present day, the fund of the national originalities remains strong and irreducible. There is no question of one country being more or less merged in the other. It does, then, look as if the two peoples, growing aware of the justifiable amount in their mutual claims to recognition, had mentally accepted each other; and that acceptance, as it lies at the root of their political understanding, makes them acknowledge that they can roughly complete each other—an admission equivalent to the perception of a spiritual affinity. Thus it is that artistic examples and patterns are freely sought by one with the other, and that, with the present eclectic freedom of taste, they show parallel growths in most literary fields.

But what English and French literatures have become to each other, is yet no departure from the normal experience of the past. There is nothing in that relationship which transcends the plane of the interdependence, familiar to history, between neighboring civilizations. Are there any reasons to believe that this plane might be transcended? Can the facts of to-day be regarded as an omen of the more pronounced development that would take place in the future, should the trend toward cosmopolitanism make itself felt somewhat longer?

If the causes which have favored of late the growth of an international culture continue to operate, the close dependence and analogy between the literatures of England and France will at least remain what it is, and probably become more marked. Their connection with the national organisms that sustain them would remain intimate and essential; but as it is assumed that the increasing resemblance between the English and the French civilizations would preclude wide divergences in the social and the moral life of the two countries, it would, however, be possible for their literatures to be mainly swayed by waves of psychological influence, the character and origin of which would not be strictly national.

This is, in fact, what is already taking place. The existence of an international literature chiefly postulates that the emotions and interests of men were become in a large measure supra-national; and the present years are showing us, more decidedly than ever before, just this shifting of the center of preoccupations with the cultivated public of England and France.

The case would be different, if through their inner development English and French literatures were still in the first phases of their normal growth; they might then be expected to show those marked departures and turns which constitute the rhythm of literary progress. The fact that both England and France have reached a stage of slackness in that respect, makes it unlikely that they should witness such wholesale changes, as from classicism to romanticism, and the reverse. The age of synthesis is that of relative stability.

National differences of civilization being to a large extent merged in one common way of living, the waves of influence which stirred the minds and hearts of men and women would not usually belong to one nation, but sweep over larger fields. One should thus expect to see France and England feeling in common the stress of those European or world currents, the trend of which would be to certain subjects and moods, and as a consequence, towards such or such technique and form. Themes would be in the air, suggested by the drama of human life in its eternal aspects, but colored by the changing light which the progress of civilization threw upon the ever-present problems. Such are the anxious thoughts which even now are engrossing the mind of the post-war world, and the echo of which can be heard in the novel and the drama and the poetry of France and England: the preoccupation with the future of the race, the hope of peace, the crisis of democracy, the social conflict, the sexual question, the impatience of human imagination with the bounds of our physical domain, and the unsatisfied satiety of the seeker for new impressions. It is not to be expected, or indeed desired, that the care of form should lose its privileged rank among the motives of the literary artist; but the response to life growing as it were more wide and deep with the writer, the matter of his work would tend to receive more stress than its manner; and literature, without being merged in philosophy, morals and drama, would grow more definitely, even in its lighter moods, philosophical, ethical and dramatic.

At any rate, and if we may indulge a little longer in this playing with possibilities, the natural grouping of writers would be common to both countries.

The days are over of the literary schools, more or less self-organized on the basis of an implicit allegiance to a set of principles. The only unifying force, in the endless variety of individual reactions, is now the affinity of temperaments. Freedom being a privilege of the artist, the choice of form is no longer of supreme importance; writers must be classified, according to their mood and art first, and in the second instance only to their style. Now, mood and art are international, whilst style and expression, being necessarily bound up with language, are more narrowly entangled with the nation. So the lines of psychological affinity, instead of being accessory to the imperious demands of nationality, would cut across the frontiers; the preference of inspiration and art over style as a principle of grouping would create families of artists, on a more than national basis. Language, and the national spirit, being thus dispossessed of their primacy in literature, the passing from the old order to the new would be thereby effected, in so far as the art of writing was concerned. The only other condition is that a sufficiently wide public should be able to read works indifferently in one language or the other; for outside of the minds that can enjoy it, literature is an abstraction; and little would it matter that writers were cosmopolitan, if readers in a decisive majority were not.

Now it is safe to assume that the proportion of the cultivated public to which in both countries works written in the other language are accessible, has not ceased to grow. It does not keep pace, however, with the spread of the taste for reading in these democratic days. As for translations, they are a most useful compromise, and have played a part of immense magnitude in the diffusion of the cosmopolitan spirit; the comparative history of literature rightly stresses their importance. If the intellectual nationalities of Europe have learnt to understand and interpenetrate one another, and if they have been, in the process, brought to some extent nearer a common central position of partly international culture, it is owing in the first instance to translations. Their increased number is at present and will be more and more an efficient means toward the further advance of the international ideal. But technically they belong, as works of art, to one language and one literature; they do not lift the whole matter onto a different plane.

The probabilities of the future, however, are outlined in the facts of to-day. Already groups of writers, defined according to the reality of their inspiration and art, stretch across the frontiers of national speech and national feeling. The circumstance is not by any means new; there were in the past individual thinkers, whose consciousness was predominantly occupied with human concerns, and who thus were intellectually nearer to the kindred spirits of other nations, than to most of their own compatriots; and there always were imitators, who reproduced the art of a foreign artist. Cosmopolitan tendencies, indeed, have always been at work. The sign of the times is that the internationally-minded man of letters is now much more frequent, that the unattached elements of his consciousness are more numerous and essential; lastly, that his technique is not necessarily one of imitation, artistic impulses of similar kinds springing up at the same time, and independently, in various countries, and the generation of art being no longer supremely national, but rather international. It is impossible to tell whether the French "surréalistes," or their English correlatives, first put to practice the principle of discontinuity; to all appearances, the technique was in the air, and cropped up everywhere. The most substantial assurance of the European culture which is coming, is that the seed of new literary formulæ, as of new schools of painting and music, of new scientific theories, are scattered over the Continent and grow in several countries at once. Very obviously Somerset Maugham as a playwright and novelist is nearer to the French "Théâtre Libre" and to Maupassant than he is to Barrie; there is more analogy between Lytton Strachey and André Maurois, than between Maurois and Duhamel; Thomas Hardy, novelist and poet, should be classed with Maupassant and Claudel, not with Galsworthy. . . . There has ceased to be, in mere nationality, a massive force so overpowering as to outweigh at once analogies of temperament and art; and the conditions of our days are working back to those of the middle ages, before the national complex became predominant among the impersonal elements in an artist's consciousness.

Still, the linguistic barrier seems to remain insuperable. The instrument of literature being necessarily language, its medium is not a creation of the writer's will, but a social fact, inseparable so far from the life of a national group. An international literature, in the full meaning of the term, would imply a world fused thoroughly enough into one political state, to have adopted one language, and endowed it with the rich associations of a mother tongue. Such a consummation is not only very distant, it is at present unlikely. We should not hastily pronounce that it is unthinkable: who can set a limit to the changes of the future, and to the plasticity of the human genius? But beyond the stage of the United States of Europe, our imaginations may for some time at least refuse to go; the welding of that heterogeneous mass into a single whole, unified enough to have one mental life and one language, is a prospect at present allowed only to the Utopian. So far as our conceptions can usefully stretch, there will thus enter into the expressions of a writer, however cosmopolitan his intellectual tastes may be, that powerful flavor of nationality which breathes in the sounds and radiates through the images that the men and women of a country have spoken and called up for ages. Poetry, in this respect, is even more national than prose; it relies to a greater extent on the subtle power of words, the magic of images and the spell of syllables. In every way, then, nationality of language, and through it nationality of spirit, is an essential factor of the literary work. Second only to the temperament of the artist in importance, it is easily first among the other elements of his personality. It will very long—perhaps forever—remain the most abundant source of variety in literature, next to the originality of the individual writer.

It would take the fanaticism of a zealot not to rejoice that it should be so; that in the cosmopolitan world of to-morrow, logic and fact should equally point to the survival of nations, living organisms, from which the larger body of mankind will draw its life; from the fruitful diversity of which the range of inspiration and effect in international literature will be supported and extended. One language intimately possessed must be the instrument of the artist in words; and that there should be several languages, is inevitable so long as the full cycle of intellectual activities is run on a national basis. Languages can, to some slight extent, influence each other, and even be brought nearer by syntactical analogy; but a unification of languages is clearly impossible; to make them one is to kill all to the benefit of one. Mankind, in its wise maturity, may well ponder before it takes such a step. Solutions that reconcile the uniformity of a practical instrument with the variety of mother tongues, have often been sketched out, and this is no time to dwell upon them.

But since differences of nationality and language are probably to remain with us, can the present condition of things be materially altered? And would it not be more honest to say that a European literature was an impossibility?

There does not seem to be any serious objection to the phrase, so long as its meaning is not unduly stretched. It is likely that the course of events is leading Europe and the world to new experiments in the free association of human groups. Our imaginations will have to be reconciled to more supple ideas than those which were derived from the hard and fast realities of the past. That Great Britain, belonging as she does to her Commonwealth of Nations, and gradually adapting her mental outlook to her position as a world power, should yet hold her place some day in that federal union of Europe which may be more than a dream, and take her part, as she does now, in a more definitely established European culture, might well appear a paradox; still, this paradox is on a fair way to becoming a fact. It is reasonable to expect that the future will solve many antitheses, and reconcile many incompatibilities, in the more spiritual plane onto which the life of man seems to be gradually lifted. The idea of a broad cultural unit, covering a very large area with no well-defined frontiers, and including various nationalities and languages, is yet to us unfaniliar; we think rather of such groupings as primarily political, and so bound by the most definite limits. But one mode of combination does not exclude the other; and after all history shows us precedents of both.

The whole matter is in part, confessedly, a question of words; but the mere term "nationality" should not stand in the way. The analogy of provincial life in present-day nations may serve our purpose. What would happen in the cosmopolitan world which we try to figure, is not very widely apart from what is taking place to-day within some nations, like Belgium or Switzerland, where linguistic groups of roughly equal importance are associated, or others, like France, in which local dialects are regaining some literary activity. There, the difference of language, deep as it cuts, does not exclude the feeling of a common culture; neither does it, to some extent, between the English and the French-speaking districts of Canada. A broad unity of suggestion, inspiration and art can be superimposed upon the relative autonomy of provincial or dialectal literatures. In the same way, one may imagine great currents of feeling and thought playing over the frontiers of states and of languages, and the unity of a common intellectual life, of common interests, of the larger and higher preoccupations of man, being reflected through various national groups in diverging lines, those divergences resulting from the individualities of writers, even more than from their characteristics as members of a national set. There would not be one authoritative center only, from which the magnetism of artistic initiative would radiate; but the life of literature would be manifold and spontaneous, occasional points of greater influence and more intense discovery appearing now here now there, as the temperaments and original gifts of races and distinctive groups expressed themselves. From the centers where the new mood or the new technique had appeared, it would diffuse itself indiscriminately over the more passive sections of the public. This would not greatly differ from the ordinary course of things in a given nation, where initiative is vested in few and usually scattered individuals or sets, and the several districts, classes or psychological types follow suit more or less willingly and rapidly. To put it broadly, the scale of the process would be changed, rather than its nature. National genius would remain as precious an element of the fertility of the whole, as provincial inspiration should ever be, and begins to be more often, in the somewhat over-centralized literatures of England and France. And whatever revival of the local spirit present-day Europe may show, would be encouraged, not checked, by a growing cosmopolitanism of taste; it is the nation that tends to a stiff uniformity of standards, within itself as well as against the looser unity of a broader human grouping; the relaxed pressure of nationality would spell more freedom for the province or the dialect, just as it would open the way to a freer association of national cultures.

It seems hardly necessary to add that such a co-operation of national originalities would not work, unless the very feeling of nationality ceased to regard itself as exclusive. Whenever it is jealous, and brooding stubbornly upon its wrongs, or aggressive, and bent upon material expansion, the forcefulness of its claim destroys that psychological freedom which is necessary to the growth of international interests. Peace among the nations, through some sort of agreement, is a condition of the new cultural order. In spite of the crisis that has recently threatened their existence, and of the consequent narrowing of their outlook, France and England, in their mutual intercourse and in their dealings with the world, are showing themselves able of that measure of detachment, without which there is no hope for the higher destinies of mankind.

Such is, perhaps, the lesson and significance of the relative harmony that a long evolution on increasingly similar lines has created between the literatures of England and France. In their interrelation may be perceived the faint outline of the supple association which should, if the future of Europe and of the world is to evolve in a sphere of peace, link up the various selves of distinct nations in a free voluntary alliance. Just as English and French literatures preserve their independent existence in the close sympathy, mutual exchange and general likeness that bind them together, European countries would keep their separate personalities in the development of thought and letters through a morally unified Europe. But if there is genuine acceptance all round, and a fair amount of good will, with some honest interest in the response of other minds to the common problems, the practical agreement of France and England will be intensified and generalized in the new harmonious civilization to which our hopes are working out. So much may be read, perhaps, in the silent acquiescence of two nations, equally proud of their distinctive characters, but open to other claims than their own, and lending themselves, not unwillingly, to a crucial experiment in the spiritual progress of the world.

Date Due

JAN 1 0 '60			
JA 4 '66			